The Greater Mysteries of

the Divine Trinity, the Logos-Word and Creation

RON MACFARLANE

Published 2015 by
Greater Mysteries Publications
Mission, BC, Canada

Cover Design: Ron MacFarlane

Printed in the United States of America

ISBN:
ISBN-13: 978-0994007728
ISBN-10: 0994007728

DEDICATION

To my spiritual teacher, St. John the Beloved,
for his steadfast support and inspiration,
despite my many imperfections.
Also, my deepest gratitude
for all that he has done over the centuries for humanity
in his incarnations as Hiram Abiff, Joshua, Lazarus-John, Floris,
Christian Rosenkreutz, the Count of Saint-Germain and Master
Rákóczi. And most especially, for his great service
to the salvational mission of Christ-Jesus
as his appointed overseer
of esoteric Christianity.

CONTENTS

THE GREATER

MYSTERIES

INTRODUCTION

* The Two Streams of Christianity: Exoteric and Esoteric

THOUGH IT MAY come as a surprise to many, Christianity never began as a single religious institution; but in fact there were two powerful streams of Christian development that have flowed down through the centuries and which issued from the same illustrious fountainhead—Christ-Jesus.

During his life on earth, Christ-Jesus made it unequivocally clear that he intended to reveal "mysteries of heaven and earth" that had long been kept secret from mankind: "I will explain mysteries hidden since the creation of the world" (Matt 13:35). What is also clear from scripture is that these revelatory mysteries were conveyed by Christ-Jesus in two very distinct ways: to his close disciples he spoke plainly and directly; to the general public he spoke in easier-to-understand parables and stories.

> Then the disciples came and said to him, "Why do you speak to them in parables?" And he answered them, "To you it has been given to know the secrets of the kingdom of heaven, but to them it has not been given ... This is

i

why I speak to them in parables, because seeing they do
not see, and hearing they do not hear, nor do they
understand." (Matt 13:10, 13)

The revelatory teachings of Christ-Jesus, then, were wisely
separated by him into "greater mysteries" that were directly
taught only to sufficiently enlightened disciples, and "lesser
mysteries" that were allegorically taught to the unprepared,
general populace.

It is important to note that the terms "greater" and
"lesser" in no way imply "superior" and "inferior." All
mysteries established by Christ-Jesus and associated with the
Triune God are equally deep and profound. Furthermore,
being connected with the highest reality, all Christian
mysteries have efficacious power to revivify our bodies,
sanctify our souls and beatify our lives. "Greater" is only
meant to describe mysteries that are greater in depth, breadth
and complexity (and therefore more difficult to comprehend
without adequate preparation). "Lesser" is only meant to
describe mysteries that are less-detailed, intricate and
demanding (and therefore much easier for the less-educated
to understand).

After the death, resurrection and ascension of Christ-
Jesus, his bifurcated mystery-teachings became more
formalized and institutionalized. St. Peter was entrusted by
our Saviour to establish a universal *religion* and *theology* in order
to preserve, guard and disseminate the lesser mysteries of
Christianity. St. John the Evangelist was similarly entrusted to
establish a universal *philosophy* and *theosophy*[1] in order to
preserve, guard and disseminate the greater mysteries of
Christianity.

Since the lesser mysteries of Christianity are purposefully
intended for mankind in general, the universal religion (and
theology) established through St. Peter can be termed,
"outer" or "exoteric Christianity." Since the greater mysteries
of Christianity are purposefully intended for select advanced

disciples who are prepared to delve deeper into the secrets of existence, the universal philosophy (and theosophy) established through St. John can be termed, "inner" or "esoteric Christianity."

Even though both streams of Christianity are intended to be complementary and mutually beneficial, during previous centuries, powerful and corrupt authorities within the universal Church of St. Peter have been brutally intolerant of religious diversity: including Judaism, Islam, as well as esoteric Christianity. Historical expressions of true esoteric Christianity, such as the Knights of the Holy Grail and the Fraternity of the Rose-Cross, were consequently driven underground for refuge and safety. Throughout this time, esoteric Christianity has been forced to be hidden and secretive, though it was never intended to be so.

* The Gradual Public Release of the Greater Mysteries of the Son

The hidden sources of esoteric Christianity have been intentionally silent on most of the greater mysteries for the past 2000 years. While Church persecution was certainly a factor, the primary reason was the fact that the lesser mysteries of the Son, as delineated by exoteric Christian theology, were intellectually sufficient for most believers during that time. Moreover, mysteries such as the Trinity, the Logos-Word and the creation of the universe have been traditionally regarded as matters of faith revealed in scripture and not as mysteries that were knowable by unaided human reason, or that were capable of logical demonstration once revealed. Consequently, there was little intellectual interest with Christian theologians in particular and humanity in general to delve deeper into greater mysteries in a philosophical or theosophical way.

However, since the end of the nineteenth century, the intellectual development of mankind had reached the stage of advancement that necessitated the gradual dissemination of the greater mysteries. Authentic sources of esoteric Christianity began to increasingly share their wealth of mystery-wisdom with the general public. The Anthroposophical Society, founded in 1912 by Austrian philosopher and Rosicrucian initiate, Rudolf Steiner (1861-1925), is one such significant expression of modern-day esoteric Christianity.

Today, primarily because of the spiritual-scientific foundation of anthroposophy, the "greater mysteries of the Son"—out of the hidden sources of esoteric Christianity—can begin to be intellectually understood and openly conveyed in clear, logical concepts. In harmony with exoteric Christian theology, it is philosophically recognized that certain mysteries—such as the Trinity of divine persons: Father, Son and Holy Spirit—are incapable of being logically deduced by reason alone. Esoteric Christianity nevertheless maintains that once they have been divinely revealed, mysteries such as these *are* capable of logical demonstration.

While the profound Christian mysteries that are philosophically and theosophically delineated here in *The Greater Mysteries of the Divine Trinity, the Logos-Word and Creation* will undoubtedly meet with initial opposition from exoteric (Church) theologians, this new knowledge is in no way a threat to, or a diminishment of, traditional Christian doctrine. Over time, it will be recognized that these greater mysteries of esoteric Christianity positively complement and spiritually enhance the lesser mysteries of Church theology (as they were originally intended by Christ-Jesus to do).

CHAPTER 1

BEFORE THE BEGINNING:
THE DIVINE NATURE OF GOD IS SPIRIT

1.1   The Divine Nature: What is "It"?

WHILE THE EXISTENCE of God can be determined with intellectual certainty and even though many of the attributes of God's nature can be readily ascertained through logic and reason, the divine essence itself is much more "inexpressible, incomprehensible, invisible and ungraspable" to the human intellect. What is "it" that is infinite, eternal, immutable, perfect and so on? Understanding "it"—God's essential nature—requires supersensible knowledge and experience, divine revelation, as well as rational intellection since "it" is beyond the reach of the entire universe.

Analogously, we can know a great deal about invisible energy by its effects, but what exactly *is* energy? Simply giving names to the various forms of energy, such as heat, light, electricity and magnetism still doesn't say what energy is. Nor does describing the movement of energy in waves or as particles; what is "it" that travels this way? Moreover, as demonstrated by Einsteinian relativity theory, energy and matter are interconvertible; that is, energy can become matter and matter can become energy. So is energy a kind of matter? If so, then what is matter, a kind of energy? Obviously such reasoning goes around in circles and still does nothing to reveal what energy is.

Similarly with God and the universe, it is futile to describe each in terms of the other; such as "God is a superior kind of universe" or "the universe is a limited form of God." This won't tell us exactly what the divine nature is in itself.

As with invisible energy, the best that the human intellect can do regarding the transcendent divine nature is to acknowledge that it exists by virtue of its cosmic effects and to give it a name—"spirit." Spirit, by definition then, is the substance of the divine nature; it is what God is made of.

1.2   Matter, Energy, Mind and Spirit

In an intellectual effort to answer the question—"What is spirit?"—it's necessary to begin by examining matter and energy. Before we can appreciate what spirit *is,* one helpful strategy is to understand what it is *not.*

From the experiments of physical science, we know that matter is a condensed form of energy and that small amounts of matter will convert into huge amounts of energy. This fact has been thoroughly demonstrated by atomic detonation. Conversely, energy can be regarded as a rarified form of matter which no longer has mass or sensory visibility. Both matter and energy, as empirically observed, are in continual motion. Physical matter may appear at rest, but the underlying nuclear particles that comprise the various states of matter are constantly moving. Potential energy, may also appear to be at rest, but it is better understood as energy in restraint; that is, energy whose movement is subdued and held in check without being entirely stilled.

The observable differences in states (or phases) of matter and forms of energy are due entirely to the frequency of vibration (or energy levels). Liquid matter vibrates faster than solid matter and gaseous matter vibrates faster than liquid matter. In addition to the three familiar states of matter, physical science has also artificially produced exotic states of matter such as high-energy plasma (the material of stars), which is super-heated matter and which vibrates much faster than gaseous matter. Cooling matter to extremely low temperatures has also produced an exotic state known as a Bose-Einsteinian condensate.

Physical science has also identified a number of different forms of energy, such as thermal energy, electrical energy, chemical energy, radiant energy, nuclear energy, magnetic energy, sound energy, mechanical energy, elastic energy and luminous energy. As with matter, the various forms of energy are characterized by differences in their frequency of vibration. This phenomenon is particularly evident with the electromagnetic spectrum of radiant energy. The forms of energy that extend along this spectrum are radio-wave radiation, microwave radiation, infrared radiation, visible light radiation, ultraviolet radiation, x-ray radiation and gamma radiation. The energy of radio-wave radiation has the lowest frequency of vibration, which continuously increases up to gamma radiation, which has the highest frequency of vibration. All forms of energy move at tremendously higher frequencies than do the various states of matter.

Esoteric tradition and the spiritual science of anthroposophy also describe states of matter and forms of energy that are currently unfamiliar to physical science. In Hindu philosophy, an ultra-rarified state of matter known as "akasha" is postulated to pervade universal space and to provide the underlying essence of all material manifestation. Similar to akasha, the concept of "aether" or "ether" (from

Greek: pure, fresh air or clear sky) as a higher degree of matter, has been familiar to metaphysicians since the time of the ancient Greek philosophers. Aristotle, for example, theorized that the heavenly spheres were composed of aether, a fifth material substance (the "quintessence") which was distinct from earth, water, air and fire. The Renaissance physician and esotericist, Robert Fludd (1574–1637), later described the aether as a substance that was "subtler than light."

Esoteric ether is, of course, not identical to the "luminiferous ether" that was hypothesized by nineteenth-century science as the universal medium of light-wave propagation. Prior to this, Isaac Newton had also theorized about an "aethereal medium" that was finer than air, which remained in a vacuum once the air had been removed and which transmitted vibrations of light and heat. As stated in *Opticks* (1704):

> And is not this Medium the same with that [Aethereal] Medium by which Light is refracted and reflected, and by whose Vibrations Light communicates Heat to Bodies.

Unlike the theory of a luminiferous ether, however, Newton envisioned the motion of light energy as particles passing through the aether, rather than as waves propagated in a medium of ether. The scientific theory of a luminiferous ether was abandoned in the twentieth century and replaced with the Einsteinian concept of "physical space" as the medium through which light energy travels.

Nevertheless, esotericists continue to maintain the existence of ether as a transitional state between matter and energy. As stated in Hermetic philosophy:

> This Ethereal Substance forms a connecting link between Matter (so-called) and Energy, and partakes of the nature of each. The Hermetic Teachings, however, instruct that this plane has seven sub-divisions ... and that in fact

there are seven ethers, instead of but one. (*The Kybalion: A Study of Hermetic Philosophy of Ancient Egypt and Greece*; 2010)

Similarly, anthroposophical spiritual scientist, Rudolf Steiner (1861–1925), describes four gradations of ether that extend beyond the solids, liquids and gases of physical matter; in order of: (1) warmth ether, (2) light ether, (3) tone (chemical) ether and (4) life ether. In addition, these etheric gradations are not simply hypothetical but can be supersensibly perceived and studied by means of initiatory development.

While ether (in its various gradations) has a much higher vibratory nature than does matter (in its three states), energy (in its various forms) has an even higher vibratory nature than matter and ether. As with ether, esotericism has traditionally described forms of energy that are beyond the range of physical science. Vedantic philosophy, Ayurvedic medicine and Yogic teaching, for example, have for centuries postulated an all-pervading vital energy called "prana" (from Sanskrit: vital life), which is regarded as necessary to sustain life. The primary source of pranic energy for life on earth is, not surprisingly, the sun.

The ancient Indian concept of prana is very similar to the ancient Chinese notion of "qi" ("chi" or "ch'i"), since qi is also understood to be a life-force that permeates and unifies all living things. As vital energy, qi is associated in humans with breathing and blood circulation. Traditional Chinese medicine, such as acupuncture, also believes that qi energy travels throughout the body in specific channels known as meridians.

Whatever the form that energy takes, esotericism maintains that although energy has a higher vibratory nature than matter and ether, it nevertheless has a lower vibratory nature when compared to "mental substance" or "mind-stuff." Though some twentieth-century scientists, such as Arthur Eddington (1882–1944) and James Jeans (1877–1946), also theorized that the underlying principle of the cosmos was a universal form of "mind," most scientists today reject such a notion. Esotericism, however, continues to teach that mind is a universal principle that is superior to matter and energy, and therefore vibrates at a much higher level.

As with matter and energy, mental substance exists everywhere in the cosmos. Mental substance differs from matter and energy in that not only is mind in constant motion, but mental movement is purposeful, meaning-filled activity. Moreover, universal mind is imbued with a much greater degree of life and consciousness—mind stuff is alive and aware. Esotericism also teaches that universal mind is not a uniform, homogenous material but that there are higher and lower gradations of mental substance. These numerous gradations can be helpfully arranged into three fundamental distinctions: (1) the plane of subconscious mind, (2) the plane of intellectual mind and (3) the plane of superconscious mind.

The lower mental planes are characterized by decreased vitality and awareness, and are therefore categorized as "subconscious" states of mind. The subconscious states of mind, as well as being more insensate, behave in a more programmed, automated manner. Consequently, this category has also been referred to as the "instinctive mind." The mental activities of the very lowest levels of subconscious mind are more akin to the blind, mechanical motions of physical energy. Likewise, the highest forms of energy, such as life-energy (prana), behave more like the purposeful, instinctual motions of subconscious mind.

The next level of universal mind is characterized by conscious, light-filled intelligent activity, and is therefore referred to as the plane of "intellectual mind" or "conscious mind." The mental activity of this level is much more mobile, animated and creative. Mentation is not rigidly programmed like the subconscious plane of mind but is capable of rapidly generating new thoughts and ideas. As matter exhibits a powerful natural propensity to particularize, to form individualized centres of activity such as electrons, protons and neutrons; and as energy exhibits a similarly strong proclivity to particularize into discrete packets of energy ("quanta") such as photons and gluons; the mental material of intelligent mind also has a fervent impulse to particularize into noetic vortices of vibration—what are commonly referred to as thoughts and ideas. As esoterically explained by Yogi Ramacharaka in *Raja Yoga or Mental Development* (2007):

> Mind-Substance in Sanskrit is called *"Chitta,"* and a wave in the *Chitta* (which wave is a combination of Mind and Energy) is called *"Vritta,"* which is akin to what we call a "thought." In other words it is "mind in action," whereas *Chitta* is "mind in repose." *Vritta*, when literally translated means "a whirlpool or eddy in the mind," which is exactly what a thought is.

Next, the highest level of universal mind substance is the plane of superconscious mind. This exalted level of mind is intensely alive and gloriously illuminated with a unitive, cosmic consciousness. Thought formations in this mental substance are powerful, sublime and enduring. These are the archetypal ideas responsible for creatively generating the multiple forms and activities of the entire physical universe. The finest gradation of superconscious mind is so supernally alive and superconsciously aware, that it manifests qualities of beingness and self-identity. Furthermore, the substance of superconscious mind has the highest vibratory nature of anything in the universe.

Beyond the vibratory level of superconscious mind is what has been historically termed, "spirit substance," or simply, "spirit." In a sense, then, spirit is an infinitely higher vibratory level of superconscious mind. Conversely, superconscious mind is a lower, finite vibratory level of spirit—and therefore is often referred to in esotericism as "spiritualized mind."

1.3   Spirit as Absolute, Infinite Mind

So, let us summarize what has been discussed thus far in this chapter section regarding the question of "What is spirit?" Energy is a higher vibratory manifestation of matter; mind is a higher vibratory manifestation of energy; and spirit is a higher vibratory manifestation of mind. Spirit, therefore, vibrationally extends beyond the region of the mind. Though the highest level of mind can in no way duplicate or vibrationally become spirit in order to understand it, superconscious mind is nevertheless aware of the existence of spirit and knows that spirit transcends its own mental substance. Mind, then, at the highest level, can truthfully declare that spirit exists.

Moreover, from what is *known* concerning superconscious mind, we can logically extrapolate what is *unknown* concerning spirit. For example, superconscious mind is aware that transcendent spirit does not share its finite limitations of space and time. Spirit substance is beyond space and time and is therefore infinite and eternal in nature. As a higher vibratory level of superconscious mind, spirit is similar to mind substance—but raised to an infinite and eternal degree. Spirit, therefore, has been esoterically termed, "absolute, infinite mind." As expressed by Yogi Ramacharaka in *The Yoga of Wisdom: Lessons in Gnani Yoga* (2013):

> Now, then—we have seen the folly of thinking of the Divine Substance as Matter or Energy. And we have come to know it as Spirit, something like Mind, only infinitely higher, but which still may be thought of in terms of Infinite Mind, for we can have no higher terms in our thinking operations. So we may then assume that this Divine Nature or substance is SPIRIT, which we may think of as Infinite Mind, for want of a better form of conception.

Moreover, the supernal life and superconscious awareness that characterizes the highest level of universal mind derives from the parent spirit substance. Spirit is not just transcendently alive, but the ultimate source of all life—it *is* infinite and eternal life. Spirit is not just transcendently aware, but the ultimate source of all consciousness—it *is* infinite and eternal consciousness. Since spirit is infinitely aware of absolutely everything, it logically follows that spirit is completely and perfectly aware of itself as well. Spirit, therefore, is pure being—supremely-realized, self-actuality.

So, in answer to the question, "What is the divine nature; that is, what is the substance of God?"—the divine nature is spirit; the substance of God is spirit. Unlike humans, who are beings that *have* a mind, the absolute, infinite mind *is* the essence of God. God does not *have* an absolute infinite mind—God *is* the absolute, infinite mind. Likewise, God does not *have* a spirit; God *is* spirit. As biblically reiterated in the Gospel of John (4:24): "God is spirit, and those who worship him must worship in spirit and truth."

CHAPTER 2

THE BREATH OF GOD MOVES ACROSS THE WATERS: THE ONE BECOMES TWO

2.1 The Vibratory Nature of Spirit

IT IS OFTEN MISTAKENLY assumed that since the divine nature is immutable, that since the divine nature cannot and does not essentially or fundamentally change, God is therefore completely immobile, totally motionless and entirely inert. This assumption is obviously incorrect for a number of reasons.

Firstly, cosmic creation is an act of divine will and, therefore, an example of God's creative activity. Secondly, a characteristic of life is incessant motion and activity, and since God is life itself and thereby the source of all life in the universe, the divine nature is also characterized by perpetual activity. Thirdly, according to the Hermetic "principle of vibration": "Nothing rests; everything moves; everything vibrates" (*The Kybalion*). This principle also applies to the divine nature; or more correctly, this principle has been universally established *by* the divine nature of God. The spirit-substance of God manifests the highest vibratory level possible; everything in cosmic creation results from a lowering of the divine vibratory level of the spirit.

Since spirit vibrates at a frequency beyond anything in the created universe, this intense movement cannot be directly perceived by any non-spiritual means. From the perspective of universal creation, spirit vibrating at transcendent rapidity appears perfectly still and at rest, what has been termed, "'the abiding peace of the Lord." As explained, once again, in *The Kybalion*:

> The vibration of Spirit is at such an infinite rate of intensity and rapidity that it is practically at rest—just as a rapidly moving wheel seems to be motionless. And at the other end of the scale, there are gross forms of matter whose vibrations are so slow as to seem at rest. Between these poles, there are millions upon millions of varying degrees of vibration. From corpuscle and electron, atom and molecule, to worlds and universes, everything is in vibratory motion.

2.2   Spirit-Force and Spirit-Substance

The transcendent vibratory nature of spirit becomes somewhat easier to comprehend once a divine activity, such as the creation of the universe, is envisioned; once "the Spirit of God moves upon the face of the waters" (Gen 1:2). Creations within the absolute, infinite mind are transcendently analogous to the mental conceptions—the thoughts and ideas—of the finite human mind. Divine ideas, however, are super-infused with life, reality, consciousness and power. Incredible to say, the universe and everything within it began as one such divine idea.

Analogous to human ideation, but of course raised to a supernal degree, the process of conceiving a divine idea within the absolute, infinite mind is esoterically understood to require a "mover" (an initiating impulse) and a "moved" (a receptive material). The divine initiating impulse is, of course, the divine will ("spirit-force"); and the responsive material is, of course, divine mind-material ("spirit-substance"). The function of the initiating force of divine will is to act as a purposeful seed-impulse to quicken and excite the divine mental material. The function of the responsive material of the divine mind is to faithfully expand and embellish the originating seed-impulse. It would be incorrect to regard one mental operation as active and the other as passive, since they both are intensely active but in unique, complementary ways.

The spirit-force of divine will does not of course exist separate and apart from the spirit-substance of divine mind. Spirit-force is best regarded as an energizing function within the perfectly amenable spirit-substance of the divine mind. Consequently, the mutual activity of spirit-force and spirit-substance establishes the vibratory nature of the absolute, infinite mind.

It's important to understand that the spirit-force of divine will is characterized by a fundamental propensity to contract inwardly, to condense towards a centre. As such, the concentrating will-force can be regarded as an essential, centripetal activity within the spirit-nature of God. The spirit-substance of divine mind, on the other hand, is characterized by a fundamental propensity to expand outwardly, to enlarge in all directions when excited by a centralized concentration of divine will. As such, the expandable mind-substance can be regarded as an essential, centrifugal activity within the spirit-nature of God. The transcendently rapid, back-and-forth rhythmic oscillation from divine centre to divine circumference (which is everywhere in infinity) establishes the vibratory nature of spirit. This vibratory movement of spirit is, of course, eternal; it had no beginning and will have no end—it is a permanent feature of spirit.

To intellectually comprehend the vibratory activity of spirit, a commonplace physical analogy may prove helpful. Imagine a long, coiled spring attached at each end to opposite walls in a room. At one end of the spring, the coils are pulled together and compressed. When released, the coils speed away from the compressed end towards the opposite wall. When reaching there, the spring rebounds back to the original end, where the coils are recompressed causing them to once again travel back to the opposite wall. The back and forth oscillation of the spring continues until it runs out of energy. In the case of spirit vibration, however, the rhythmic fluctuation can never run out of energy, and so continues indefinitely.

The centripetal action of divine will and the centrifugal action of divine substance perfectly complement each other. The compressive action of the divine will does not continue indefinitely, but is held in check by the expansive action of divine substance. When the will-force becomes sufficiently concentrated, it spontaneously ignites the expansive activity of spirit-substance. In consequence, the will-force is impelled outwardly in the expanding spirit-substance. Likewise, the expansive action of spirit-substance does not continue indefinitely, but is held in check by the compressive action of the divine will. When spirit-substance becomes sufficiently distended, the divine will spontaneously reverses the movement back toward a concentrated centre. In this way, divine will and divine substance are held in perfect balance; neither can become a polarizing extreme. Moreover, without this perfect complementary interchange, the vibratory nature of the spirit would not exist.

2.3   The Two Divine Persons

From the manner in which divine will-force and spirit-substance have been discussed thus far, these two fundamental aspects of the absolute, infinite mind will appear to be rather abstract and lifeless. Though such a simplified approach is of value in forming a basic comprehension of spirit vibration, further understanding imbues spirit-force and spirit-substance with divine reality and divine life.

We know from what has been said thus far that spirit or divine nature is pure, actualized existence and that it is perfectly real and totally alive. God, therefore, possesses all the properties and features of "personhood," though raised of course to an unimaginable, infinite degree. What is an essential aspect or principle of the absolute, infinite mind is likewise supremely real and alive with unique characteristics of personhood. Divine will-force and spirit-substance, then, are transcendently imbued with divine reality and life. As such, they are more accurately understood to be divine persons, rather than as just two impersonal principles of mentation within the absolute, infinite mind. We can truthfully say, then, that within the one nature of God there are two divine persons. This is not to suggest, of course, that there are two separate Gods. There can be only one supreme reality, but that reality innately manifests as two divine persons.

Moreover, the oscillating activity of spirit vibration is infinitely far from being a simple, mechanical-style, back-and-forth interchange. It is actually a fully real and life-filled personal interaction of deep and intimate mutuality between two divine persons. Using the familiar language of human gender, the divine person whose centralizing will-power provides the initiating seed-impulse for spiritual mutuality has been esoterically referred to as the "Divine Masculine," or more personally as the "Heavenly Father." Likewise, the divine person who receptively multiplies, develops and outwardly expands upon the concentrated will-impulse of the Heavenly Father has been esoterically referred to as the

"Divine Feminine," or more personally as the "Holy Mother."

The use of gender terms in connection with the two divine persons is certainly not meant to impose the characteristics of human sexuality on the divine nature. As discussed previously, the divine nature infinitely transcends all human attributes, including sexual distinction. God, therefore, cannot be described as "male," "female," or "androgynous," in the way that these terms are applied to human beings. Nonetheless, it would be equally incorrect to say that the divine nature is entirely "genderless." It would be more accurate to say that the divine nature includes all positive aspects of human sexuality, but raised to the degree of infinite perfection. More accurately understood, the human sexual distinctions of male and female are finite, imperfect reflections of the two divine persons. As conveyed in biblical scripture: "God created man in his own image, in the image of God he created him, male and female he created them" (Gen 1:27). From this we can also deduce that human sexual intimacy was divinely intended to mirror the sacred mutuality of the Heavenly Father and the Holy Mother.

2.4 The Universal Principle of Gender

Since the entire universe is an incomplete, imperfect reflection of God's nature, the perpetual, mutual interchange between the Heavenly Father and Holy Mother is partially and finitely manifested throughout the entire cosmos. This divine mutuality is particularly expressed in the vibratory nature of all matter, energy and mind. Within cosmic creation, then, the divine persons manifest in a limited capacity; not as persons, but as universal gender principles: the "universal masculine principle" and the "universal feminine principle." These two fundamental principles underlie and direct all phenomena and activity in the universe.

As parent-principles, the universal masculine principle can also be termed the "father-principle" of cosmic creation, and the universal feminine principle can also be termed the "mother-principle" of cosmic creation. In the Hermetic philosophy of *The Kybalion*, the "principle of gender" is recognized as one of the seven fundamental axioms of the universe: "Gender is in everything; everything has its Masculine and Feminine Principles; Gender manifests in all planes."

The Chinese philosophical notion of yin and yang (taiji), and the familiar Taoist symbol (taijitu: see Figure 1 below), similarly attempt to conceive and convey the universal principle of gender. As concisely explained by Aaron Hoopes in *Zen Yoga: A Path to Enlightenment through Breathing, Movement and Meditation* (2007):

> The Taijitu is one of the oldest and best-known life symbols in the world, but few understand its full meaning. It represents one of the most fundamental and profound theories of ancient Taoist philosophy. At its heart are the two poles of existence, which are opposite but complementary. The light, white Yang moving up blends into the dark, black Yin moving down. Yin and Yang are dependent opposing forces that flow in a natural cycle, always seeking balance. Though they are opposing, they are not in opposition to one another. As part of the Tao, they are merely two aspects of a single reality. Each contains the seed of the other, which is why we see a black spot of Yin in the white Yang and vice versa. They do not merely replace each other but actually become each other through the constant flow of the universe.

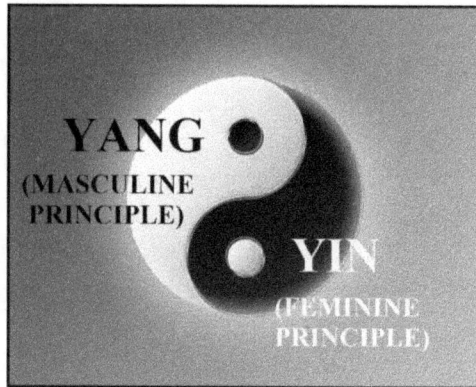

Figure 1: The Taoist Taijitu Symbol

Unfortunately, by strictly associating positive qualities and phenomena with the yang or masculine principle (such as day, light, hard, hot, aggressive and good); and negative qualities and phenomena with the yin or feminine principle (such as night, dark, soft, cold, passive and evil)—this black-and-white, polarizing conception has been historically used to justify male domination and female subjugation in Oriental society. Such a misinterpretation is clearly a deliberate distortion of the true creative functions of both universal gender principles.

The universal feminine principle, rather than being a negative, passive, imitative function is instead the fertile, generative, productive function throughout cosmic creation. While the fecund and procreant function of the universal feminine principle is excited and initiated by the fructifying function of the universal masculine principle, the superabundant phenomena of the cosmos is the labour and handiwork of the mother-principle.[2] This fact has been instinctively recognized in everyday language by the term,

"Mother Nature," when applied to universal creation. As echoed in *The Kybalion*:

> The part of the Masculine principle seems to be that of directing a certain inherent energy toward the Feminine principle, and thus starting into activity the creative processes. But the Feminine principle is the one always doing the active creative work—and this is so on all planes. And yet, each principle is incapable of operative energy without the assistance of the other. In some forms of life, the two principles are combined in one organism. For that matter, everything in the organic world manifests both genders—there is always the Masculine present in the Feminine form, and the Feminine present in the Masculine form.

As indicated in *Zen Yoga* above, the principles of yin and yang, the mother-principle and the father-principle, constantly strive for balance. In Taoist philosophy, this mutual impulsion for balance is not regarded as a distinct universal force or principle. In Christian esotericism, however, a third fundamental principle is held to exist between the two universal parent-principles: the "principle of harmonious balance" or the "principle of balanced union." As with the mother-principle of cosmic creation and the father-principle of cosmic creation, the "son-principle" (as the third intermediary universal principle) is an imperfect, finite manifestation of a third, intermediary divine person—known esoterically as the "Eternal Son."

CHAPTER 3

LET THERE BE A UNION OF LOVE:
THE TWO BECOME THREE

3.1 The Third Divine Person

TO REPEAT, the divine person of the Father fundamentally manifests the initiating, spiritual will-power of the absolute, infinite mind. The divine person of the Mother fundamentally provides the expansive, generative spirit-substance of the absolute, infinite mind. In Latin, the word "substance" means "standing under." This of course is equivalent to the English word, "understanding." In this sense, then, spirit-substance is equivalent to spiritual understanding. In other words, the substance of God is the "understanding" of God; that is, the "wisdom" of God. In short, then, the Heavenly Father is the divine personification of the will-nature of the absolute, infinite mind. The Holy Mother is the divine personification of the wisdom-nature of the absolute, infinite mind.

While the two divine persons are of course co-existent and co-eternal, through their complete and enduring mutual interchange they are also co-equal. The divine will is perfectly suffused with divine wisdom and is therefore an omniscient will-power. The divine wisdom is perfectly suffused with divine will, and is therefore an omnipotent wisdom-substance. Moreover, though the divine will activates the outpouring response of divine wisdom, the Heavenly Father does not exist prior to the Holy Mother. Both divine persons have always existed together in eternity.

Once again, the complete mutual interchange between the divine persons is transcendently more than simply a blind, mechanical interaction. Through the ceaseless, rhythmic conjoining of omniscient will and omnipotent wisdom, the Heavenly Father and the Holy Mother are eternally united as one spirit—God. This supernal union can be analogously regarded as a divine marriage; but to a depth, an intimacy and a joy unimaginable to the human mind. The absolutely total and complete mutuality of each divine person for the other is an expression of divine love. God the Father and God the Mother are co-united in an infinite and eternal embrace. The abiding, rhythmic exchange of reciprocal love is the living pulse of the heart of God.

The reciprocal love of each divine person for the other is so tangible and so real that a third divine relation is generated from their spiritual union—the divine Son. Just as the loving mutuality of the divine Father and the divine Mother is without beginning or end, the divine Son is eternally generated and likewise has no beginning or end. In order to better convey this essential idea that the divine Son does not have a beginning but is "eternally generated" instead, Catholic teaching exclusively employs the term, "begotten," when referring to the Eternal Son. God the Son, then, is not generated but "eternally begotten."

The eternally-begotten existence of the divine Son that arises from the everlasting, mutual love of the Heavenly Father and the Holy Mother should not be understood as some form of sexual reproduction. Instead, this transcendent familial relationship within the absolute, infinite mind serves as the archetypal pattern for all generative activity throughout the cosmos—on all planes and for all manifestations of matter, energy and mind. Human sexuality is merely one imperfect, physical manifestation of the perfect mutuality of divine persons. As similarly stated in *The Kybalion*:

> This [Hermetic] Principle [of Gender] embodies the truth that there is *Gender* manifested in everything—the Masculine and Feminine Principles ever at work. This is true not only for the Physical Plane, but for the Mental and even the Spiritual Planes. On the Physical Plane, the Principle manifests as *Sex*, on the higher planes it takes higher forms, but the Principle is ever the same. No creation, physical, mental or spiritual, is possible without this Principle.

Care must always be taken when applying terminology derived from human relationships to describe the divine relationship of the three persons of God. Terms such as "husband," "wife," "marriage," "child" and "family" all have narrow, limited usage when referring to the sublime union of the Triune God. Nevertheless, it can be argued that by analogously extending the experience of ideal human relationships, human intellects can gain a valid, though circumscribed, comprehension of the threefold love of God.

As the third divine person of God, the Eternal Son is logically co-equal, co-existent and co-eternal with the Heavenly Father and the Holy Mother. The fundamental, intrinsic and living activity of the absolute, infinite mind is therefore threefold or "trinitarian" in nature. Moreover, it is not simply an interaction of three mental principles, but a loving relationship of three divine persons. Also, the Trinity of divine persons is not arbitrary or invented, but is a necessary reality of God's nature as it exists. A fourth divine person is not necessary to God's nature and therefore does not exist.

3.2   The Holy Mother and the Holy Spirit

In orthodox Christian belief, the Trinity is commonly understood as the Father, the Son and the Holy Spirit; rather than as the Father, the Son and the Holy Mother. When correctly interpreted and understood, however, the Holy Spirit is clearly the feminine person of God and, therefore, synonymous with the Holy Mother.

The original Hebrew word for "spirit," used throughout the Old Testament, is "ruach," a term with a feminine gender. Unfortunately, later Greek translations and New Testament writings used the Greek word, "pneuma," for spirit, a term that is gender neutral. Since the Holy Spirit is a divine "person" and not a "thing," the personal pronoun traditionally chosen for pneuma was "he" instead of the impersonal "it." Subsequent Latin translations also contributed to the defeminization of the Holy Spirit by using the Latin word, "spiritus," for spirit, a term that has a masculine gender. Through language, then, (and some would argue because of cultural patriarchy) the Holy Spirit in modern times was no longer understood as the feminine person of God, as the divine Mother.

Nevertheless, in Old Testament scripture, "wisdom" is often personified, feminine and given divine attributes. Since the Holy Mother (or Holy Spirit) is the divine personification of God's wisdom, certain biblical references to wisdom can easily be interpreted as early references to the Holy Spirit-Mother. In the Wisdom of Solomon (7:21–29), for example, wisdom is described as follows:

> I learned both what is secret and what is manifest, for wisdom, the fashioner of all things taught me. For in her

is a spirit that is intelligent, holy ... all-powerful, overseeing all ... For wisdom is more mobile than any motion; because of her pureness she pervades and penetrates all things. For she is a breath of the power of God, and a pure emanation of the glory of the Almighty ... for she is a reflection of eternal light, a spotless mirror of the working of God, and an image of his goodness. Though she is but one, she can do all things, and while remaining in herself, she renews all things ... for she is more beautiful than the sun, and excels every constellation of the stars.

Further supportive examples can be found in Proverbs (2:13–20):

Happy is the man who finds wisdom, and the man who gets understanding ... She is more precious than jewels ... She is a tree of life to those who lay hold of her... The Lord by wisdom founded the earth, by understanding he established the heavens; by his knowledge the deeps broke forth.

Moreover, the Greek term for "wisdom" used throughout the New Testament is "sophia," a feminine term. Even more significantly, Sophia in Greek mythology was the name of the goddess of wisdom. No doubt, early Greek readers of biblical writings would have continued to associate the word "sophia" with a divine feminine personification (though not necessarily as the Holy Mother-Spirit). Nevertheless, some early Christian writers, such as church patriarch Theophilus of Antioch (?–c.185), did clearly associate sophia-wisdom with the Holy Spirit-Mother. In the second book of his collected writings, *Apologia Ad Autolychum* (c.180), Theophilus wrote of "the Trinity of God, and His Word, and His Wisdom." The original Greek terms used by Theophilus were "Theos," "Logos" and "Sophia."[3] Also noteworthy, Theophilus was the first known theologian to actually use the word, "Trinity," when referring to the three persons of God, since the term was not used in the Bible.

The word, "wisdom," is often used synonymously for intelligence, knowledge, understanding and of course truth. By referring to the Holy Spirit as the "spirit of truth," certain biblical passages establish a logical association between the Holy Spirit and the feminine Sophia-wisdom. In the First Letter of John (4:7), for example, it states that "the [Holy] Spirit is the witness, because the [Holy] Spirit is the truth." Also in the Gospel of John (14:16, 17), in speaking to his disciples about the Holy Spirit, Christ-Jesus declared that the Father God "will give you another Counselor, to be with you forever, even the Spirit of truth." Paul, in his First Letter to the Corinthians (2:7–13) also associated the Holy Spirit with wisdom and truth, as indicated in the following passage:

> [W]e impart a secret and hidden wisdom of God, which God decreed before the ages for our glorification ... God has revealed to us through the [Holy] Spirit. For the [Holy] Spirit searches everything, even the depths of God ... So also no one comprehends the thoughts of God except the [Holy] Spirit of God ... And we impart this in words not taught by human wisdom but taught by the [Holy] Spirit, interpreting spiritual truths to those who possess the [Holy] Spirit.

As the preceding examples clearly indicate, then, it is not unreasonable to conclude from biblical scripture that the Holy Spirit, as divine wisdom and truth, is the feminine person of God; that is, the Holy Mother.

3.3 The Trinity as Father, Son and Holy Mother

The ideas of a maternal Holy Spirit and a Trinity of Father, Son and Holy Mother are not just recent, novel conceptions. Some powerful Church figures in the early years of Christianity held similar notions. The translator of the Latin Vulgate, Jerome (347–420), for example, wrote:

> In the Gospel of the Hebrews that the Nazarenes read it says, "Just now my mother, the Holy Spirit, took me." Now no one should be offended by this, because 'spirit' in Hebrew is feminine, while in our [Latin] language it is masculine and in the Greek it is neuter. In divinity, however, there is no gender. (*Jerome's Commentary on Isaiah II*)

Also, second-century Church leader, Clement of Alexandria (c.150–c.215), wrote:

> And God Himself is love; and out of love to us became feminine. In His ineffable essence He is Father; in His compassion to us He became Mother. The Father by loving became feminine: and the great proof of this is He whom He begot of Himself [the Son]: and the fruit brought forth by love is love. (*Who is the Rich Man that Shall be Saved*; Chap. 37)

The assertion of Christian esotericism that the Holy Spirit is best understood and referred to as the Holy Mother does not mean, of course, that the absolute, infinite mind is entirely feminine in nature. It is not a statement that God is exclusively "Mother." Nor does belief in the divine person of the Holy Mother lead to, or promotes, a form of "goddess worship." The one God is the perfect union of three divine persons. By virtue of this divine triune nature, God eternally exists in a transcendent state of absolute, harmonious unity. All three divine persons, then, are necessary for God's complete existence.

Moreover, recognizing the divine person of the Holy Mother does not erroneously supplant the person of the Father with the person of the Mother. Each person of the

Trinity, though co-equal and consubstantial (of one and the same substance, essence or nature), remains distinct from the other. Each divine person cannot become another divine person. In God, there cannot exist three divine Fathers, or three divine Sons or three divine Mothers. Moreover, co-equally expressing the divine nature of the other person does not result in a personal transformation. For instance, there are numerous biblical examples of the Heavenly Father expressing maternal affection, but that in no way eradicates the necessary existence of the Father. A similar understanding has been expressed in the *Catechism of the Catholic Church* (*CCC* 239):

> By calling God "Father," the language of faith indicates two main things: that God is the origin of everything and transcendent authority; and that He is at the same time goodness and loving care for all His children. God's parental tenderness can also be expressed by the image of motherhood (Isaiah 66:13; Psalm 131:2) which emphasizes God's immanence, the intimacy between Creator and creature. The language of faith thus draws on the human experience of parents.

The biblical passages referred to in the *Catechism* which indicate the expression of maternal tenderness by the Heavenly Father are the following:

> For thus says the LORD ... As one whom his mother comforts, so I will comfort you. (Is 66:12–13)

> O LORD, my heart is not lifted up, my eyes are not raised too high; I do not occupy myself with things too great and too marvelous for me. But I have calmed and quieted my soul, like a child quieted at its mother's breast; like a child that is quieted is my soul. (Ps 131:1, 2)

3.4 The Holy Spirit-Mother and Cosmic Creation

While feminine or maternal qualities have been properly associated on occasion with the Heavenly Father, masculine characteristics have also been associated with the Holy Spirit, the divine Mother; though in this case, often incorrectly. Particularly within creation, the universal feminine principle—as a temporal manifestation of God the Mother—provides the underlying, material substance and the ever-active, creative impulse towards variety and multiplicity. The universal feminine is truly the working principle of creation. As such, the Holy Spirit (being the divine source of the universal feminine principle) is assumed to be "masculine" and referred to as "he," due to the mistaken gender stereotype that power and activity are strictly male characteristics.

It's important to understand that even though the divine will is the primary manifestation of the Heavenly Father, all divine and cosmic expressions of activity and power are not exclusive manifestations of the divine masculine person or the universal masculine principle. All persons of the Trinity actively share the divine will, but in three distinct ways. Though the universal masculine principle provides the initiating will to create, the real labour of developing and establishing the details of creation is accomplished by the will-direction of the universal feminine principle. The familiar saying: "A father works from sun to sun, but a mother's work is never done," equally applies to the universal feminine principle as it does to human mothers.

As the ultimate source of the universal feminine principle in the cosmos, The Holy Mother-Spirit has a more intimate and immanent relationship with universal creation,[4] while the Heavenly Father has a more observational and transcendent relationship with universal creation. The intuitive acknowledgement of this divine maternal immanence in

Nature has found popular and accurate expression in terms such as "Mother Nature" and the "womb of Nature." Though pervasively present—through the Eternal Son—in creation, it is important to remember that as an eternally co-existent person of the Trinity, the Holy Mother is not confined to creation, but also extends infinitely and timelessly beyond it.

It is also esoterically significant that the English word, "mother," and the English word for physical substance, "matter," are both derived from the same Latin word, "mater." The Holy Spirit-Mother, as the eternally real personification of wisdom, is the "understanding" or "substance" of the absolute, infinite mind. Physical matter is a reduced cosmic manifestation of spirit-substance, the Holy Spirit-Mother. Physical matter, therefore, is not the Gnostic antithesis of spirit and inherently evil, but is instead "densified spirit"; that is, spirit-substance at a slower degree of vibration. To denigrate and disparage the matter-foundation of the created universe is to mistakenly and disrespectfully mistreat the cosmic, substance-body of the divine Mother.[5]

3.5 The Familial Relationship of the Trinity

While exoteric Christianity has been willing to acknowledge that God can certainly express divine maternal love, it currently does not agree with esoteric Christianity that the Holy Spirit is the divine person of the Mother. Mainstream Christianity continues to associate a masculine gender with the Holy Spirit. Not surprisingly, then, exoteric Christianity and esoteric Christianity have different understandings of the Trinity of divine persons and their supernal relationship to each other.

In the Roman Catholic doctrine of the Trinity, the Father

"eternally begets" the Son, and the Holy Spirit "proceeds" or is "spirated" by the combined action of the Father *and* the Son. Eastern Orthodox doctrine varies slightly by asserting that the Holy Spirit proceeds from the Father *through* the Son. From the order of begetting and proceeding, then, both doctrines view the Father as the "First" Person of the Trinity, the Son as the "Second" Person of the Trinity and the Holy Spirit as the "Third" Person of the Trinity.

As understood by esoteric Christianity, however, the divine person of the Father and the divine person of the Mother have necessarily co-existed in spirit from eternity. Both divine persons are, then, the "primary" or "first two" persons of the Trinity. Accordingly, the Holy Spirit-Mother does not "proceed" or "spirate" from either the Father or the Son or from both. Also, since the divine Son is eternally begotten from the mutual love of the Heavenly Spirit-Father and the Holy Spirit-Mother, the Eternal Spirit-Son can be transcendently regarded as the "divine progeny" or the "divine child" of the two divine parents. As such, the divine Son in esoteric Christianity can be regarded as the "secondary" or "third" person of the Trinity.

The terms, "primary" and "secondary" do not, of course, suggest that any one divine person is more important than another. Nor do the terms imply a temporal order, of one divine person existing before another. Each person of the Trinity is co-existent, co-eternal, co-equal and consubstantial. The terms are only of value in understanding the relationship of the three divine persons to each other. In a transcendent sense, the Trinity is a "family" of divine persons perfectly united in spirit.[6]

3.6 The Spirit-Nature of God *is* Divine Love

From what has been conveyed thus far regarding the

transcendent, familial interaction of the Heavenly Father, the Holy Mother and the Eternal Son, it is clearly evident that divine love pervades the entire Trinitarian relationship. So much so, that a logical conclusion of this understanding is that divine love is an essential quality of God's spirit-nature; that, in fact, divine love *is* the spirit-nature of God. In other words, "divine love" is synonymous with "spirit," which is synonymous with "absolute, infinite mind."

As with humanity's initial knowledge of the Trinity, the certain knowledge that "God is love"— that the spirit-nature of the Absolute One is divine love—initially came as a revelation from Christ-Jesus. Like the Trinity, the knowledge that God is love cannot be established by logical reasoning alone. But as here demonstrated, once the Trinity is revealed and intellectually understood, the love-filled nature of God can then be logically deduced.

It is also important to keep in mind, of course, that since it is synonymous with spirit and absolute, infinite mind, divine love is equally transcendent and mysterious. Stating the knowledge that "God is love" in no way indicates that divine love is entirely understood. Logically considered, to completely understand God, one must completely understand divine love; and to completely understand divine love, one must completely understand God.

3.7 Diagrams of the Heavenly Father, the Holy Mother and the Eternal Son

Diagrammatically,[7] the distinctness and interrelationship of the three persons of the Trinity can be understood as follows:

WILL

(goodness)   (mercy)

HEAVENLY
FATHER

WISDOM   (compassion)   LOVE

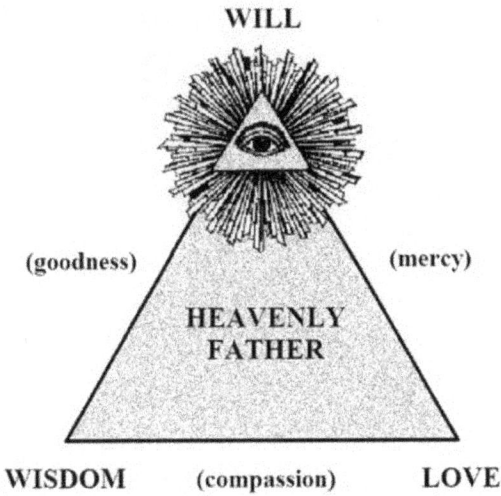

Figure 2: Diagram of the Heavenly Father

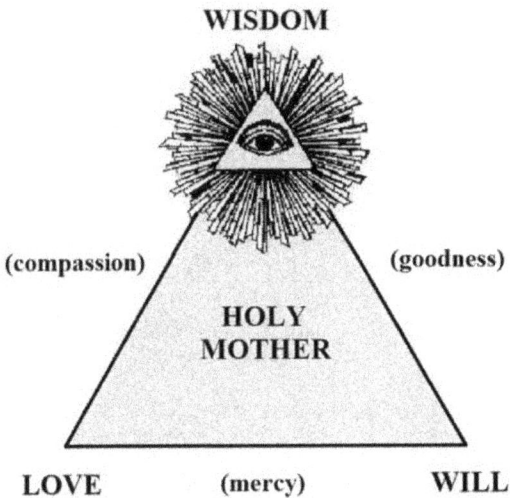

WISDOM

(compassion)   (goodness)

HOLY
MOTHER

LOVE   (mercy)   WILL

Figure 3: Diagram of the Holy Mother

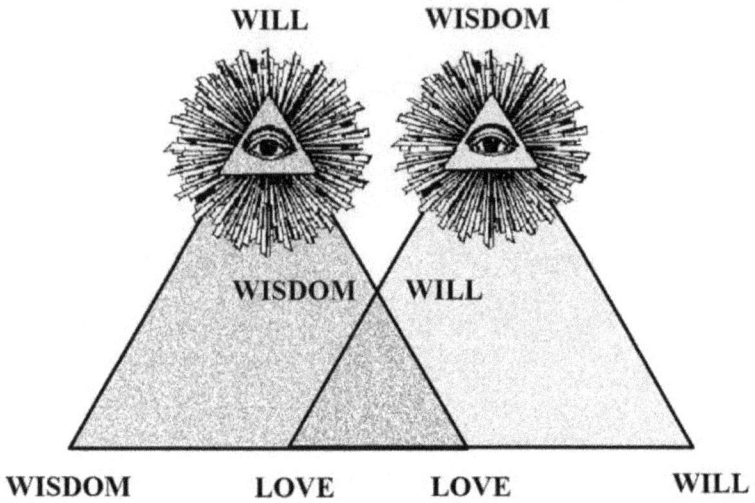

Figure 4: Diagram of Divine Mutuality

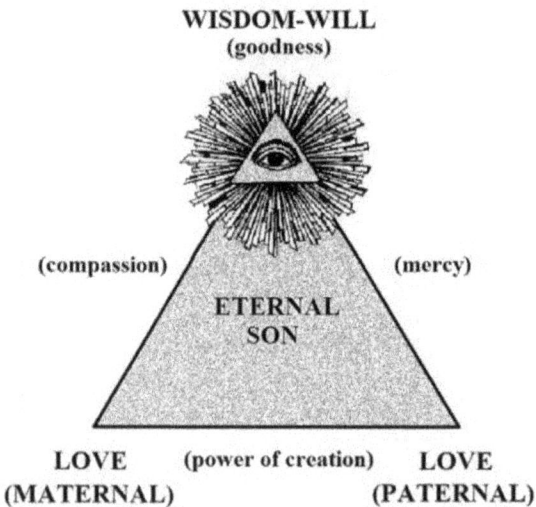

Figure 5: Diagram of the Eternal Son

Since all three divine persons are co-equal and consubstantial, the Heavenly Father, the Holy Mother and the Eternal Son each include and express divine will, wisdom and love. However, God the Father, by nature, manifests the divine will primarily, and divine love and wisdom secondarily (see Figure 2). God the Mother (the spirit of truth), by nature, manifests divine wisdom primarily, and divine love and will secondarily (see Figure 3).

When the two parent-persons conjoin in a mutual indwelling of divine love (rhythmically consummated throughout eternity), then the divine Son is eternally actualized from their perfect union (see Figure 4). As the child of mutual love between God the Father and God the Mother, and as the supernal unification of divine will and wisdom, the Son-God personifies perfect harmony, balance and equanimity. As such, the Son-God manifests unified will and wisdom (goodness)[8] primarily, and conjoined maternal and paternal love secondarily (see Figure 5).

Also of profound significance, the transcendent conjoining of the maternal love of the Holy Mother and the paternal love of the Heavenly Father imbues the Eternal Son with the divine power of creation. The two parent-persons of God, therefore, do not create;[9] but rather, eternally beget—and *only* beget the divine Son. The person of God the Son does not beget, but instead has the infinite power to create.

Associating distinctive characteristics and functions for each divine person of the Trinity, such as the primacy of will, wisdom or love, is correct Trinitarian "appropriation" as long as it is understood that each divine person shares these characteristics and functions, and always acts together in unison. As concisely expressed in the Athanasian Creed: "We worship One God in Trinity and Trinity in Unity, neither confounding the Persons nor dividing the substance." It is important to keep in mind that the divine persons of the

Trinity completely interpenetrate each other. This mutual "indwelling" or "perichoresis" (from the Greek: permeation without confusion) maintains an eternal co-equality in essential nature while retaining the personal characteristics of each.

Esoteric Christianity does not subscribe to "modalism," the erroneous notion that the Trinity does not exist as three divine persons, but instead as three divine "modes" of expression. Modalism postulates that the One God only *appears* to be different divine persons depending on the specific characteristic or function being expressed. The Hindu Trimurti is one such example of modalism. In this case, Brahman, the one God, appears as Brahma when he is functioning as cosmic creator; Vishnu when he is functioning as cosmic preserver; and Shiva when he is functioning as cosmic destroyer. These three separate deities are not regarded as real divine persons, but merely as "appearances" or "transformations" of the one God, Brahman.

CHAPTER 4

THE WORD OF THE SON AS THE UNIVERSAL "I AM"

4.1 Human Self-Awareness

THE HUMAN MIND, subjectively experienced, exhibits a distinction between *being* and *knowing*, a distinction expressed in language by the terms "I," and "Am." "I" is the word-symbol of self-identity (the ego); it represents one's essential being. "Am" is the word-symbol of self-reflection, the mental capacity of knowing that the self exists.

The cognitive union of being and knowing generates self-conscious awareness. The individual ego-self, the I, not only innately exists, but through mental reflection it also consciously knows that it exists. Through self-awareness, then, the I knows that it exists as an I—it knows that it "is." Self-conscious awareness is indicated symbolically in language by the declaration, "I am."

In the evolutionary history of mankind, individuals did not always experience a strong sense of self-identity. The vast early stages of prehistoric human development (rapidly recapitulated in early childhood) were characterized by an extremely dim and generalized "I awareness." Throughout this long formative process, the personal self was not perceived as an individualized centre of consciousness and being, but much more generally as a "group self." The self was not perceived to be separate and unique; but rather, was perceived to be an integral and organic member of a family, tribe or ethnic community.

By the time of Graeco-Roman civilization, a strong sense of individual self-identity had become established in many souls. Instead of identifying the self as an Athenian or as a citizen of Rome, certain individuals could then perceive the self as an individual personality, and thereby consciously assert: "I am Plato" or "I am Caesar."

While mankind in general was increasingly developing a strong sense of separate selfhood, a few highly-advanced initiates, as far back as the Egypto-Chaldean-Hebraic cultural era, had already begun to intuitively sense a spiritual component to I awareness. Brief, blinding flashes of a higher "spiritual self" were perceived by these initiates as external, divine occurrences—not as inner soul experiences. The Hebrew initiate Moses, for example, as recorded in Chapter 3 of Exodus, experienced the resplendent consciousness of the higher self, the "cosmic I AM," as the voice of Yahweh-God speaking from a "flame of fire out of the midst of a bush [that was] not consumed."[10] It was only through the later incarnation of Christ-Jesus that it became possible for human beings to experience the spiritual I AM internally, within the human soul.

4.2   Divine Self-Awareness

The absolute, infinite mind, as the ultimate source of all finite mind-stuff and mental activity in the universe, not surprisingly exhibits a similar distinction between being and knowing; but unlike the ephemeral and transitory human mind, these twin distinctions are supernally real and alive. Within the absolute, infinite mind, "being" is a divine person—the personification of "supreme-being"—also known esoterically as the Heavenly Father. "Knowing" is likewise a divine person—the personification of "all-consciousness" —esoterically known as the Holy Mother.

Otherwise understood in terms of the spirit nature of God, the supernal state of supreme-being is achieved by the inward, centripetal contraction of the spirit towards an infinite centre-point. When infinite spirit contracts and draws its entire nature toward a centre-point of existence, it becomes pure actuality. Likewise, the supernal state of all-consciousness is achieved by the outward, centrifugal expansion of the spirit towards an infinite circumference. When infinite spirit expands and distends its entire nature towards a periphery of existence, it becomes pure awareness.

At the ultimate point of contraction, spirit is completely inward-directed and self-focused, but not self-aware. Likewise, at the ultimate periphery of expansion, spirit is entirely outward-embracing and unfocused in extended consciousness, but not self-aware. Divine self-awareness arises from the vibratory oscillation between spirit contraction and spirit expansion. In other words, the constant back-and-forth interchange of divine being (self) and divine knowing (consciousness), necessarily generates divine self-awareness. Moreover, it logically follows that perfect, divine self-consciousness is the exact, harmonious balance of divine being and divine knowing (as illustrated in Figure 6 below). Correspondingly, moving in either divine direction away from the precise mid-point of spirit vibration necessitates a diminution of divine self-consciousness.

Divine Self-Consciousness

Divine Being ←————————————→ Divine Knowing

⌈ The Self of God: ⌉   ⌈ The Consciousness of God: ⌉
⌊ Heavenly Father ⌋   ⌊   Holy Mother   ⌋

The Eternal Son

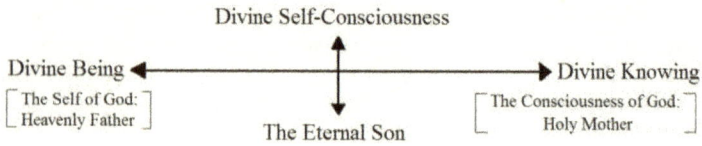

Figure 6: Diagram of God's Self-Awareness

In less abstract, more personal terms, the mutual spirit interchange between the divine being of the Heavenly Father and the divine knowing of the Holy Mother necessarily generates (begets) the divine self-awareness of the Eternal Son. Alternatively expressed in a still more comprehensive way, the Eternal Son is understood to be the real personification of God's perfect awareness of himself.

In any effort to humanly comprehend the vibratory nature of divine spirit, it is fundamentally important to keep in mind that spirit *moves* with such transcendent rapidity as to be simultaneously at complete and perfect rest. Consequently, the eternal and infinite spirit oscillation from pure being to pure consciousness occurs with such incomparable celerity that spirit is *simultaneously* self-actualized, self-aware and all-conscious. In a supernal sense, then, the Heavenly Father, the Holy Mother and the Eternal Son are simultaneously separate *and* perfectly united in spirit. Analogously, at a human level, this triune condition would be mundanely similar to being totally awake, completely asleep and busily dreaming—all at the same time!

As human parents affectionately see themselves reflected in their child, the "fruit of their union," on the supernal level of divine existence, the Heavenly Father and the Holy Mother consciously "self-know"[11] each other through the self-awareness of the eternally-begotten Son.

Since the divine offspring is the perfect union of the paternal love of the Heavenly Father and the maternal love of the Holy Mother, the Eternal Son is in a transcendent sense "androgynous," perfectly uniting the procreant, generative power of both divine parents. Consequently, from the Son of divine self-awareness flows the deific power to create; that is, to mentally "conceive" divine ideas and thoughts within the absolute, infinite mind. The mental creations of the Eternal Son, acting in Trinitarian unity with the Heavenly Father and the Holy Mother, are necessarily imbued with spiritual reality and life, quite unlike the ephemeral thoughts of the finite human mind.

4.3   The Creation of the Logos, the Divine Self-Concept

The primary and highest mental conception generated by the Eternal Son is, of course, the "idea of God," the divine self-concept. As a mental creation of the absolute, infinite mind, the idea of God is a mental image or reflection of the one nature, and certainly not a replication or duplication of the One God (which is logically impossible). The divine self-concept can be described as the pre-eminent thought-expression ("Logos" in Greek) of God's self-awareness—the Eternal Son. Moreover, the Logos is transcendently analogous to the human thought-expression of self-awareness—"I am."

The supreme idea of God, the Logos, is therefore esoterically regarded as the "Great I AM." Moreover, as God's foremost thought-expression, the Logos has also become esoterically known as the "Universal Word," since human thought-expressions can similarly be formed into abstract "words." Since the divine self-concept logically flows from divine self-awareness, the Universal Word is correctly regarded as the first-born creation of God the Son (acting in Trinitarian unity with God the Father and God the Mother).

It is important to note, that as the first-born mental

conception of the Triune God, the Universal "I AM" Word is not an additional divine person; but rather, is a created being; in fact the primary and foremost created being in the mind of God. Moreover, as the divine self-concept, the Universal Word is the spiritually created "image" or "likeness" of God the Son. As the highest possible spiritual reflection of God the Son, the Great I AM Word is a god-like being infused with universal life and reality, and therefore is also esoterically referred to as the "Universal Being." As a divine creation, the Universal Being is of course limited and has a beginning, unlike the Supreme Being of God. In a very real sense, then, the Universal Being can be regarded as the finite and temporal "countenance" or "face" of the infinite and eternal God.

4.4 The Relation of the Logos-Word to God the Son

From what has been conveyed thus far, it should be clear that esoteric Christianity does not consider the Word of God to be synonymous with God the Son, as is often the case with exoteric, mainstream Christianity. For example, the *Catechism of the Catholic Church* (479) states:

> At the time appointed by God, the only Son of the Father, the eternal Word, that is, the Word and substantial Image of the Father, became incarnate.

Nevertheless, esoteric Christianity certainly recognizes that there is a profound and intimate relationship between the divine self-concept (the Universal Word) and divine self-awareness (the Eternal Son). This transcendent connection is understood to be spiritually real and alive, between creature and Creator; or more personally expressed, between the first-born child of God and the divine parent of God the Son (see Figure 7 below).

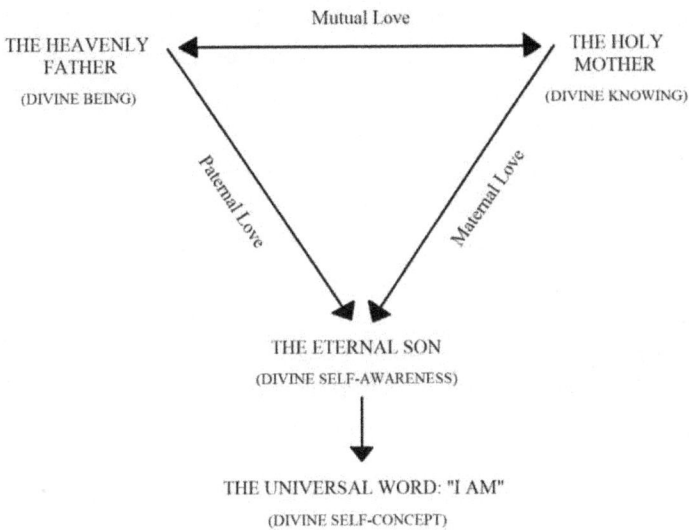

Figure 7: The Conception of the Universal Word

4.5 The Universal Word According to the Gospel of John

St. John the Evangelist concisely concentrated the greater Christian mysteries of the Universal Word in the opening lines of his gospel: "In the beginning was the Word, and the Word was with God, and the Word was God. The same was in the beginning with God." As indicated by St. John, the Word is a created being having a beginning; otherwise he would have written, "*Before* the beginning was the Word" or "*From eternity* was the Word."

Numerous biblical commentators mistakenly assert that the phrase, "In the beginning," used by Moses in Genesis and St. John in his gospel, means "In eternity." Each of these writings, however, is referring to the creation of the universe and the creation of mankind—both of which had a beginning.

Since God has no beginning or end, the phrase "In the beginning" is obviously referring to universal creation, not to the pre-existent Creator. At the start of creation, then, the Word was "called into being" by God.

The differentiation of the Word as a separate being created by God, and not pre-existing as a divine person, is further emphasized by the following gospel phrase, "and the Word was with God." In order to be "with God," it is logically necessary to be separate and distinct *from* God. The concluding phrase of St. John's opening sentence, "and the Word was God," though appearing to contradict what has been said thus far, continues to be entirely consistence when properly understood.

According to esoteric Christianity, identifying the Word *with* God by stating, "and the Word *was* God," does not mean that the Word is co-equal, consubstantial and co-eternal with God; that is, that the Word is a divine person of the Trinity. Exoteric, mainstream Christianity, however, has historically considered the Word to be synonymous with the person of God the Son. But even in limited human experience, a "word" is a mental creation, the direct expression of a person—not the actual being of a person. However, given the intimate association and connection of self-consciousness and self-conception, even in human cognitive experience, any miscomprehension, misconception or confusion is certainly understandable. A few suggested alternative phrases which would convey an equivalent (but less contradictory) esoteric meaning are as follows:

- "and the Word was the idea of God"
- "and the Word was God conceived"
- "and the Word was God's conception of himself"
- "and the Word was the image (form, face, countenance) of God"

The second sentence at the beginning of St. John's

Gospel, "The same was in the beginning with God," further supports the esoteric Christian understanding of the Universal Word when correctly interpreted. With this particular enigmatic translation, the word "same" is commonly understood to mean "the same thing"; that is, "The same thing (Word) was in the beginning with God." With this interpretation, however, St. John's sentence comes across as a bland, pointless repetition. However, there are much more esoterically meaningful synonyms for the word "same": such as "self-same, identical, duplicate, copy, look-alike, image or likeness." St. John's sentence, then, can be more cogently understood to say that "The image and likeness of God was in the beginning with God." Once again, as the image and likeness of God, the Word is correctly understood to be a divine creation, a perfect reflection of the divine Creator, but not to be a divine person.[12]

4.6 The Universal Word as the Image and Likeness of God

In conventional theology, the familiar phrase, "the image and likeness of God," has traditionally been ascribed exclusively to Adam, the original biological ancestor of all mankind, brought into being on the sixth day of creation. As stated in Genesis:

> Then God said, 'Let us make man in our own image, after our likeness' … So God created man in his own image, in the image of God he created him … the Lord God formed man of dust from the ground, and breathed into his nostrils the breath of life, and man became a living being. (Gen 1:26, 27; Gen 2:7; RSVCE)

The Hebrew name for earth or ground is "adamah," hence the name of "earthly man." As well, in biblical Hebrew, "Adam" was also used to refer to mankind in general and not just a single individual, as evidenced from the following passage:

> In the day that God created man, in the likeness of God made he him; male and female created he them; and *blessed them, and called their name Adam*, in the day when they were created. [emphasis added] (Gen 5:1–2; KJV)

In this sense, then, all mankind was created in the image and likeness of God (at least in the beginning).

Additionally, in the mystic and esoteric traditions of East and West, there is postulated a "cosmic Adam" that exists distinct from, and antecedent to, the "earthly Adam" (mankind). This primal, macrocosmic or "archetypal man" is termed "Adam Kadmon" in the Jewish mystical writings of Lurianic Kabbalah. The Hellenistic Jewish philosopher, Philo (c.30 BC–c.50AD), was, however, the first known ancient writer to use the expression, "heavenly man," which he described as:

> [B]eing born in the image of God, has no participation in any corruptible or earthlike essence; whereas the earthly man is made of loose material, called a lump of clay." (*De Allegoriis Legum*)

In esoteric Christianity, then, the Primal Man, the First Adam, is not a single human being but a macrocosmic, universal being created in the image and likeness of God—the same being referred to as the Word or Logos. Moreover, in a very real sense, as the perfect image and likeness of God, the Universal Word is the mirrored "face" or "countenance" of God. By means of the divine self-concept of the Logos, the divine self-awareness of God the Son is made known, the invisible spirit of God is made visible, the formless spirit of God is given form. He who has seen the Word, knows the Son; and he who knows the Son, understands the nature of the Triune God.

4.7   The Primal Man—the Universal Word—in Sacred Literature

The existence of a single, primal, universal created being that stands as intermediary between God and the rest of creation is an ancient notion that has taken various conceptual forms throughout history—the idea of the Logos, for example. Despite many philosophical differences, the Logos was fundamentally conceived to be the primary intermediary between God and the world, through whom God created and governed the entire cosmos.

To Plato, the Universal Logos was termed the "World Soul" (the "Anima Mundi" in Latin), which he described as follows:

> Therefore, we may consequently state that: this world [universe] is indeed a living being endowed with a soul and intelligence ... a single visible living entity containing all other living entities, which by their nature are all related. (*Timaeus*; 4th century BC)

To eminent Pre-Socratic philosopher, Heraclitus (c.535–475 BC), the Logos functioned as the underlying rational order of the universe, but was more of a universal principle of intelligence than an intelligent, universal being.[13] Somewhat later, as previously mentioned, Philo conceived the Logos as a single, universal being whom he designated the "heavenly Adam" and "the man, the word of the eternal God."

Prior to the birth of Christ-Jesus, Hebrew scholars had also seriously entertained the notion of a divine mediator between God and creation. In this case, a distinction was established between Yahweh-God and the Word of Yahweh. In Aramaic, the Word of God was called "Memra." While some scholars regarded the Memra-Word as just another substitute name (like "Adonai") for the unutterable name of

God (the "Tetragrammaton"), others held the view that Memra was a distinctive persona of Yahweh by which he created the world and reveals himself to mankind, as indicated in Psalm 33:6: "By the word of the LORD the heavens were made, and all their host by the breath of his mouth." Moreover, the Memra-Word was even considered by some pre-Christian Hebrew sages to be the anticipated Messiah who would take flesh and dwell among his people.

Gnostic literature postulated a concept similar to Philo's Primal Man, which was termed "Anthropos." To Gnostic teacher, Valentinus (c.100–c.160), Anthropos described the archetypal or supernatural essence of humanity. According to Church Father, Irenaeus (c.115–c.202), other Gnostics believed that:

> [T]he Primal Father of the Whole, the Primal Beginning, and the Primal Incomprehensible, is called Anthropos ... and that this is the great and abstruse mystery, namely, that the power which is above all others and contains all others in its embrace is called Anthropos. (*Libros Quinque Adversus Haereses*)

Similarly, in certain Hindu philosophy, Brahman, the absolute, infinite and unchanging reality, gives rise to the primordial being, Hiranyagarbha (the "golden fetus"), who is regarded as the fountainhead of the created universe. In the *Upanishads*, Hiranyagarbha is called the "soul of the universe." Similarly postulated in other Hindu philosophy is the idea of "Purusha," which in Sanskrit translates as "Cosmic Man." In Sutra literature, Purusha is the universal self that pervades the entire cosmos.

In certain Yogic teachings, the World Soul or Universal Self is termed the "Universal Life," and is regarded as a fundamentally important cosmological concept, explained as follows:

Many writers have spoken of the Universal Life, and the

One [God] as being identical—but such is a grievous error, finding no warrant in the Highest Yogi Teachings. It is true that all living forms dwell in, and are infilled with the Universal Life—that All Life is One. We have taught this truth, and it is indeed Truth, without qualification. But there is still a Higher Truth—the Highest Truth, in fact—and that is, that even this Universal Life is not the One, but, instead, is in itself a manifestation of, and emanation from [or mental conception of], The One ... "Spirit" which we called "The Absolute," expressed itself in the Universal Life, which Universal Life manifested itself in countless forms of life and activity ...

[W]e would say to you that the emanation [or mental creation] of the Absolute is in the form of a grand manifestation of One Universal Life, in which the various apparent separate forms of life are but centers of Energy or Consciousness. (Yogi Ramacharaka; *Lessons in Gnani Yoga*, 1934)

Moreover, in certain Rosicrucian teachings, the Universal Self or World Soul is also regarded as a fundamentally important cosmological concept, indicated by the following:

But it must be always noted that in the Secret Doctrine of the Rosicrucians the World Soul is not regarded as the Infinite Reality, but merely as the First Manifestation thereof, from which all subsequent manifestations proceed and into which they are finally resolved. The World Soul is not Eternal, but, on the contrary, appears and disappears according to the rhythm of the Cosmic Nights and Days ...

The Rosicrucians further hold that it is not correct to think of the World Soul as having been created "out of nothing" by the Eternal Parent, and still less to think of it having been created from the substantial essence of the Eternal Parent by division, separation, or partition (such ideas being held to be logically impossible and fallacious). On the contrary, it is held that the World Soul exists as an IDEA of the Eternal Parent. (Magus Incognito; *The Secret Doctrine of the Rosicrucians*; 1949)

4.8   Two Different Creation Accounts of the Universal Man in the Bible?

At first, the Mosaic account of creation appears to be somewhat different from St. John's Gospel version of events; though in fact, it is merely different language for identical ideas. In Genesis (1:3), the first creation of God on Day one was supernatural light: "And God said, 'Let there be light' ["Fiat lux" in Latin]; and there was light." This light was clearly a sensory-imperceptible, non-physical light since it was created prior to the sun, moon and stars on Day four, as indicated from the following:

> And God said, "Let there be lights in the firmament of the heavens to separate the day from the night; and let them be for signs and for seasons and for days and years, and let them be lights in the firmament of the heavens to give light upon the earth." And it was so. And God made the two great lights, the greater light to rule the day, and the lesser light to rule the night; he made the stars also. And God set them in the firmament of the heavens to give light upon the earth, to rule over the day and over the night, and to separate the light from the darkness. (Gen 1:14–18)

The supernatural light called into being at the dawn of creation is clearly the "light of universal reason"—the Logos. What Moses terms "primal light," St. John calls "the Word"; both writers are referring to the same event.

CHAPTER 5

THE LOGOS-WORD AS THE LORD OF THE UNIVERSE

5.1 Through the Universal Word All Things Were Made

AS THE FIRST-BORN, divine idea conceived within the absolute, infinite mind, the Logos-Word—the Universal I AM—is the wellspring of all further creation. The universe was not created apart from the Universal Word; but rather proceeded from it, and within it. All subsequent creation is logically a diminution of this supreme idea. Moreover, as the truest and highest mental image of God, the Universal Word faithfully reflects the life and reality of God, the will, wisdom and love of the divine parent. The Universal Word, then, is the foremost created being, and not simply an impersonal, universal manifestation.

Through and by means of the divine self-concept, the Universal I AM, God the Son (acting in Trinitarian unity) establishes, shapes and governs the development and activity of the entire created universe. As unequivocally stated by St. John: "all things were made through him [the Logos-Word], and without him was not anything made that was made. In him was life ... (Jn 1:3–4). Regarding the manifested universe, then, the spirit of God (in the person of the Son) acts through the creative will of the Universal I AM.

The greater mysteries to unravel at this point are how exactly does the created universe proceed from the Logos-Word, and how is it that the one Universal Life became many lives?

5.2   The Lowering of Spirit Vibration and the Macrocosmic-Adam

The conception and formulation of all divine thought and ideation within the infinite mind of the Absolute necessitates a diminishment of spirit vibration. Of course any reduction in spirit vibration, no matter how infinitesimally subtle, results in an immediate lowering from the level of the infinite and eternal to that of the finite and the temporal. Nevertheless, a divine idea is as indestructible and as everlasting as God wills it. For as long as a divine idea is held in the absolute, infinite mind it partakes of the reality of God; that is, it is infused with consciousness and life.

The idea of God, the divine self-concept, is logically the subtlest and finest reduction of spirit vibration possible. While obviously not pure spirit, the Universal I AM is supernally spirit-like, the closest creation possible to God; not God, but the god-man, the Macrocosmic-Adam. To the Macrocosmic-Adam, the pure spirit of God exists vibrationally above and beyond him. While God is self-existent and real by his own divine nature, the Macrocosmic-Adam has reality by virtue of God's existence. As the perfect image and likeness of God, the Macrocosmic-Adam "mirrors" the reality of God within his own vibrational nature. In this way God is "present" to the Macrocosmic-Adam, as his transcendent source of reality, which is experienced as his true self. To God, then, his self-conception is below his infinite nature; but to the divine self-concept—the Macrocosmic-Adam—God (though present to him in consciousness) is infinitely beyond his own created nature.

As the first and foremost reduction of spirit vibration, any further decrease in vibration must obviously be done by lowering the vibratory level of the Logos-Word; that is, decreasing the vibratory nature of the Macrocosmic-Adam. The rest of the universe results, in fact, from further lowering the vibratory level of the Logos-Word. All else in the universe must, therefore, exist at a lower vibratory level than the Logos-Word.

5.3 The Logos-Word and the Dawn of Creation

At the dawn of creation, the Logos-Word vibrationally descended out of the infinite and eternal spirit. Esoteric tradition has long held that the primordial birth of the Logos-Word was in the manner of a macrocosmic awakening from a deep, divine sleep in which it had always existed. As described in *The Secret Doctrine of the Rosicrucians*:

> The World Soul, at the Dawn of a Cosmic Day, may be said to be like a dreamer freshly awakened from a deep sleep, and striving to regain consciousness of himself. It does not know what it is, nor does it know that it is but an Idea of the Eternal Parent. If it could express its thought in words it would say that it has always been, but had been asleep before that moment. It feels within itself the urge toward expression and manifestation, along unconscious and instinctive lines—this urge being a part of its nature and character and implanted into it by the content of the Idea of the Eternal Parent which brought it into being.

In further esoteric detail, at the instant of its awakening, the newborn Logos-Word opened to the blinding light of cosmic Day—the radiant reality of the Son-God. It immediately drew into itself, as its first cosmic breath, the life-giving power of the Son. Innately perceiving its entire pristine nature nakedly exposed to the all-seeing "I" (self-awareness) of God, the nascent Universal Word protectively drew into itself, into its own nature—in an involuntary, instinctual effort to wrap itself in comforting darkness, desperately trying to return to the soothing shadow of unconscious sleep within the womb of spirit.

Vibrationally speaking, by contracting inwardly in an effort to withdraw from the full intensity of the Spirit-Son, the newborn Word increasingly lowered the vibrational level of its own nature. The result was indeed a plunge into darkness—not the veilment of divine sleep, however, but the black shroud of dense matter.

As previously stated in *The Secret Doctrine of the Rosicrucians*, at the dawn of creation, the newborn Word was immediately aware of its eternal parent, but was initially overpowered by the dazzling radiance, the full reality, of the Son-God. Moreover, though the Primal Word was "God-conscious" in the beginning, it was not "self-conscious" of its own primordial nature. By increasingly lowering its vibratory nature, the innate God-consciousness of the Primal Word was correspondingly diminished and darkened. This vibratory descent, of course, did not continue forever, but in a relatively short period of time[14] reached a nadir of decline, after which the vibratory level began to increase.

5.4 The Great Manifestations of Universal Mind, Energy and Matter

In God's case, absolute, infinite mind is not something

distinct from him or something that he possesses; it is his actual spirit nature, "that which he is." With human beings, however, we often make a distinction between the mind and the person. We don't usually think of the mind *as* the person; but rather, the mind is something that the person possesses. Similarly with the Logos-Word, though its essential nature is a supernal degree of mental substance that innately possesses life, consciousness and being, esotericists often make a distinction between the Universal Person (the Logos-Word) and the universal mind (the first manifestation of the Logos-Word). The nature of the Logos-Word, as the intermediary between absolute, infinite mind (spirit) and universal mind can be accurately termed, "spiritualized universal mind."

When the Primal Word began to contract inwardly at the dawn of creation, this lowered the vibrational level of its essential nature, resulting in a diminishment of its inherent God-consciousness. Esoterically, the process and result of lowering the vibratory level of Word-substance is termed a "manifestation," rather than a "creation." Creation refers exclusively to the process and result of conceiving a divine idea within the mind of God. In esoteric Christian terminology, then, God the Father and God the Mother *eternally beget*; God the Son *creates*; and the Logos-Word *manifests*.

The first manifestation of the Primal Word is "universal mind." Universal mind is not a separate being or a duplicate universal person. It belongs to the Primal Word; in fact, it *is* the Primal Word in a diminished capacity. It is important to understand, at this point, that it is not quite accurate to say that in the beginning universal mind pervaded the entire universe. It is more accurate to say that in the beginning, universal mind *is* the universe; since the entire universe is, in fact, the Primal Word, the Universal Person.

As the Primal Word continued to inwardly contract, universal mind correspondingly decreased through various levels of vibration; analogous to visible light decreasing in wavelength: from violet, to blue, to green, to yellow, to orange, then to red. Universal mind, then, rather than being a single, decreased vibrational level of the Primal Word is a vast range of vibrational levels that became increasingly slower and diminished in consciousness.

At a specific level of vibrational descent, universal mind became universal energy. This was no arbitrary distinction but a significant transformation of the Primal Word. Analogously, infra-red vibration is quite different from visible light vibration, even though it results from simply a continued decrease in electromagnetic wavelength. Universal energy, like universal mind, is a vast range of vibrational levels that share common characteristics.

As the Primal Word continued its downward plunge into decreased vibration and diminished consciousness, at a certain level universal energy became universal matter. Various levels of universal matter were increasingly condensed until the Primal Word exhausted its descending impulse. Universal matter at this level exhibited little vibratory movement, and no perceptible life or consciousness. As water vapour is crystallized into ice, the Primal Word at the nadir of descent had unconsciously frozen itself into a centre of cold, dark universal matter.

5.5 The Primal Plunge into Matter: The "Great Involution"

The primal plunge into super-dense matter by the nascent Word is esoterically understood to be analogous to a prolonged, focused concentration on a single point in the human mind, as in say, deep meditation. As in meditation, a person can become completely absorbed in their own thought, oblivious to their surroundings and to their own self.

In a true sense, then, the meditator can lose their self (that is, their self-awareness) in immersed, concentrated thinking.

In the case of the Primal Word, its inward vibrational contraction was achieved by unconsciously concentrating its own spiritualized mental nature to a single, central point within itself. By an effort of involuntary cosmic will, the Primal Word focused all of its supernal mental capacity on a point within itself that was farthest away from the blazing light of God-consciousness. Since the Primal Word, in a cosmic sense, became entirely "absorbed," "wrapped up" and "involved" in its own concentration (and completely oblivious to its spirit surroundings) as a result of its vibrational descent, the process of universal contraction has become esoterically known as the "Great Involution" (see Figure 8 below). As described in *Lessons in Gnani Yoga*:

> The true teaching is that the process of Involution was accomplished by a Principle [Manifestation] involving itself in the lower Principle [Manifestation] created within itself, and so on until the lowest [vibratory] plane was reached. Note the difference—"Principles as Principles" did this, and not as Individual Forms of Life or Being ... There was no "devolution" or "going down"—only an "involution" or "wrapping up" of Principle within Principle—the Individual Life not having as yet appeared, and not being possible of appearance until the Evolutionary process began. (Yogi Ramacharaka)

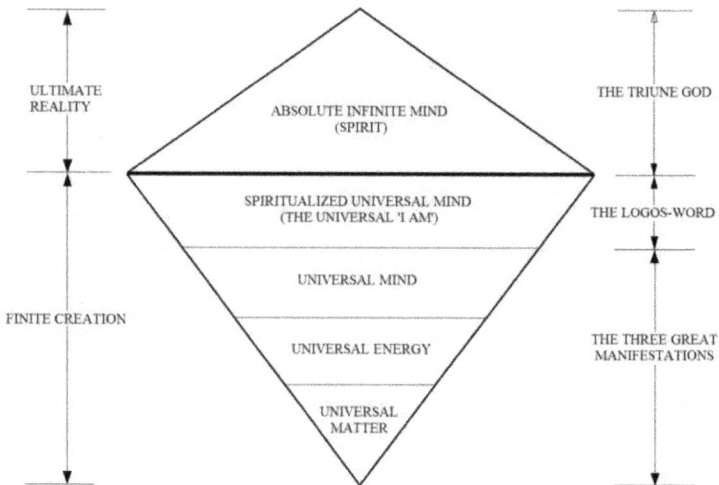

Figure 8: The Vibratory Levels of God and His Word

5.6   The "Cosmic Egg" of the Universe

Current science is at a loss to explain how the cosmic singularity—the superphysical point of origin of the entire universe—came to exist. Since the present-day universe is believed to be continually expanding after the "Big Bang" beginning, one conjecture is that the universe will eventually stop expanding and begin to collapse due to gravitational attraction. This would result in a "Big Crunch," where all matter and energy becomes compressed into a single, super-dense, super-hot and super-small point—another cosmic singularity. This process of universal expansion and contraction could theoretically go on forever, a concept known as the "Big Bounce."

While esoteric science does not entirely agree with these particular materialistic speculations, it does concur that the present material universe had a superphysical point of origin, wherein all matter and energy were compressed. However, esoteric science also asserts that all mind, life, consciousness and being were additionally enclosed and constrained within this "cosmic seed" of origin; and not by gravitational force, but by the unconscious will of the Primal Word.

The traditional Rosicrucian symbol for the nucleus of ultimate contraction that resulted from the Great Involution of the Primal Word is a circle with a black dot in the centre. The circle is figuratively referred to as the "Cosmic Egg" and the black dot is termed the "Germ within the Cosmic Egg." The cosmological notion that the material universe began as the "hatching" of a great cosmic egg is also found in numerous ancient mythologies.

For instance, in Hindu mythology, Brahma the Creator-god was called "Kalahansa," the "Swan of Eternity" since it was he who laid the "Golden Egg" of the universe at the beginning of each "Mahamanvantara," or "Great Cosmic Cycle." In Egyptian mythology, Seb (or Geb), the god of time (Chronos in Greek mythology) and of the earth, is said to have laid the "Egg of the Universe" at the centre of which gestated the sun-god, Ra. Seb's hieroglyph was a goose, and he was often referred to as the "Great Cackler." Similarly, the "Orphic Egg" in Greek mythology was the cosmic egg from which sprang the androgynous deity, Protogenus (Gk: First-born), also called Phanes (Gk: I bring to light), the source of all the other Greek gods.

To esoteric science, visualizing the involutionary stage of the universe as a cosmic egg is not primitive, simple-minded fantasy. Esotericists have long held that the early prenatal growth stages of living organisms recapitulate (in general) the vast, developmental stages of the cosmos. Despite vague scientific speculation that life can develop from inert chemicals, the biological fact remains that "all life comes from an egg," or as English physician, William Harvey

(1578–1657), is credited as stating: "Omne vivum ex ovo." The fact that all life begins as a microcosmic seed or egg is because the entire universe once began as the concentrated macrocosmic centre of the Living Word.

5.7 The Lost Word in the Grave of Universal Matter

The Great Involution of the Primal Word has also been esoterically termed, the "Great In-Breathing," since the Universal Life drew its entire nature inwardly to a concentrated centre—cosmically analogous to the human process of deep breathing, by which oxygen is drawn into the lungs and sent to the heart-centre via the blood stream. The cosmic urge to draw inwardly did not, of course, continue indefinitely; but did eventually reach a point of exhaustion, a point of extreme densification, extreme lifelessness and extreme unconsciousness. It was as though the Primal Word had indeed disappeared into a cosmic black hole.

To a supernatural observer, it would have seemed as though the Universal Life had extinguished itself, lost itself in material darkness. When the Great In-Breathing had stopped, there was the prolonged stillness of a cosmic death, as the Primal Word rested in the peace of oblivion, lost in the eclipse of self-annihilation. But within the black stillness of the universal grave, a new God-given impulse began to stir, the cosmic will to live, to be, to return to the light (of God-consciousness). Just as the primordial impulse of the new-born Word caused it to contract inwardly and begin the Great Involution away from the light of God, so too at the nadir of cosmic midnight the innate impulse to live caused the Lost Word to expand outwardly and begin the "Great Evolution."

5.8 The "Great Evolution" of the Lost Word

At the start of the Great Evolution, the Primal Word was fully engrossed, completely involved in a contracted centre of the densest possible matter. In a cosmic sense, it had "lost itself" in deep concentration. The Primal Word had thoroughly hidden itself from the light of God-consciousness. When the Great In-Breathing had ceased, there was a mighty pause, a "Great Stillness," as nothing in creation appeared to move. Then, miraculously, a new instinctual urge was kindled in the heart of cosmic darkness, the urge to seek the light, to rise up from the motionless sarcophagus of matter and shake off the thick suffocating burial shrouds of constraint.

Needless to say, the initial spark of ascent was exceedingly faint, causing little noticeable change in the cosmic core of matter. Nevertheless, the vibratory level slowly began to increase, rather than decrease, with the result that the Primal Word slowly began to expand and grow lighter and brighter. This excruciatingly gradual process of expansion continued for vast aeons of time as the Primal Word struggled to unfold what had previously been condensed, to unwrap what had previously been compressed. The Great Evolution "evolved" what had previously been "involved" during the Great Involution.

It is important to note, however, that the Great Evolution was not simply an identical "undoing" of what had been previously "done" during the Great Involution. From the very instant of the cosmic impulse to expand, there was a wondrously profound difference that characterized the entire process of the Great Evolution; and that was an innate tendency to differentiate, to particularize, to establish numerous individualized centres of motion and activity. During the Great Involution, the continuous decrease in vibration and the corresponding densification of the Primal Word was done "en masse"; the entire homogenous, undifferentiated nature of the Universal Person was involved, not simply a component or an aspect. As described in *The*

Secret Doctrine of the Rosicrucians:

> When the lowest point in the scale of Involution was reached, then the Law of Rhythm asserted itself, and the upward climb began—the first movement of Evolution began to manifest itself. And, at this precise point, there was begun the manifestation of what may be termed "individualization," or the forming of centres of activity and consciousness. The World Soul descended into the depth of Involution en masse, and then began to emerge from those depths by an apparent "splitting up" process, in which the active new-born centres of activity began to assert themselves and to move upward toward self-expression. (Magus Incognito; 1949)

With the Great Evolution, then, the single unified nature of the involuted Word began to slowly differentiate into infinitesimally small centres or vortices of activity and movement. At first these centres were few and extremely compressed and inert; but over vast stretches of time these particles grew in number and in motion. The accumulated movement of increasing numbers of elementary particles began to slowly raise the vibratory level of the condensed Word. Through the process of particularization, the macrocosmic Word was literally manifesting microcosmic copies of itself, since it too had existed as a super-small, supercondensed concentration at the nadir of involution.

Analogous to cellular replication, the Primal Word began the process of evolution by repeatedly replicating copies of itself in elementary particle form. However, the elementary particles that were manifested during the initial stages of the *first* Great Evolution (there have been subsequent ones, as will be discussed later) were far more dense and motionless than any subatomic particle existing today. Current atoms are exceedingly more complex and advanced than the primitive elementary particles of the first Great Evolution.

Nevertheless, it is still reasonably accurate to describe the completely involuted Word as the Primal Atom, the cosmic progenitor of all other elementary particles in the universe.

5.9   The Logos-Word as the Universal Androgyne

The dual processes of cosmic involution and evolution, of universal contraction and expansion, mundanely mirror the eternal rhythm of the divine parent (as discussed in Chapter Section 2.3: "The Two Divine Persons"). The inward, centripetal action of the Heavenly Father is reflected in the involutionary contraction of the Logos-Word. This innate cosmic compulsion to unite all in a centralized condition of oneness is esoterically termed, the "universal masculine principle." Likewise, the outward, centrifugal action of the Holy Mother is reflected in the evolutionary expansion of the Logos-Word. This innate cosmic compulsion to proliferate, to expand outwardly in a dispersed condition of multiplicity is esoterically termed, the "universal feminine principle."

By reflecting the spirit nature of the divine parent, these two, fundamental, universal principles are equally essential to the nature of the Logos-Word. They are in essence, God-infused. By the consummate combination of the "father-principle" and the "mother-principle" in its own nature, the Logos-Word is understood to be an androgynous creation; hence the occasional title, the "Universal Androgyne." This mystery knowledge is biblically indicated (though somewhat confusingly) in the following passage: "In the day that God created man, in the likeness of God made he him; Male and female created he them; and blessed them, and called their name Adam, in the day when they were created (Gen 5:1, 2; KJV). In esoterically interpreting this passage, Adam is of course understood to mean Adam Kadmon, the Universal Man.

Since the spirit nature of God is divine love, the spirit-like nature of the Logos-Word is "universal love." Though not infinite and eternal like the Parent-Creator, it is nevertheless "cosmic" in its range, depth and degree. As such, the mother-principle and the father-principle of the Logos-Word are not simply lifeless laws of nature, but are instead life-filled expressions of the universal love nature of the Logos-Word. While both expressions of universal love: maternal and paternal, are co-equally balanced and essential to the nature of the Logos-Word, one or the other predominates during involution or evolution. Naturally, the paternal love of the father-principle predominates during the involutionary phase; while the maternal love of the mother-principle predominates during the evolutionary phase. Since the current universe is in an evolutionary phase, human beings intuitively refer to the cosmos as "Mother Nature" or the "womb of Nature."

5.10   Cosmic Evolution and the Universal Feminine Principle

Mirroring the divine activity of the Heavenly Father, the masculine-principle of the Logos-Word provides the involutionary, condensed "cosmic seed" for universal evolution. Analogous to certain plant seeds, the cosmic seed of the Logos-Word is sown in material darkness (the "soil" of universal evolution). Likewise mirroring the divine activity of the Holy Mother, the germinating forces of the feminine-principle (inherent in the spiritually dark matter) are aroused by the cosmic seed (during universal evolution) and begin to generate a profusion of miniature copies; that is, numerous elementary, subatomic particles. The spark of life, the centralized Logos-Word concealed in the cosmic seed, is thereby gradually unfolded, which expands the universe outwardly in increased diversity and complexity. Moreover, as the plant seed strives upward towards the life-giving light of the sun, the cosmic seed of the Logos-Word strives ever upward (in vibration) towards the life-giving light of the Son-God.

By slow degrees, the elementary particles of matter become less dense, more mobile, and in conformity to the divinely-infused direction of the feminine-principle, they become arranged into increasingly complex combinations. In the process, higher and higher levels of vibration are unfolded; but not uniformly, as in the Involutionary phase. During the evolutionary phase, the universe becomes a rich amalgam of individualized centres of development that uniquely manifest increasing signs of life, consciousness and will.

While the feminine-principle of the Logos-Word predominates during the evolutionary phase, both principles necessarily interact (as essential aspects of the universal nature) in every cosmic activity, no matter how small or how great. As stated in *The Secret Doctrine of the Rosicrucians*:

> [T]here are present in All-Creation the activities of a Male Principle and a Female Principle, both Universal in Nature, Character and Extent—both Opposing [that is, Complementary] Aspects of the World Soul—which act and react, one upon the other, and thus produce all Creative Activity and the "Cosmic Becoming" of Universal Activity and Change. And the teachings also are that these Two [Gender] Principles operate and manifest upon every plane of Life, from the Sub-Mineral, on to the Mineral, on to the Plant, on to the Animal, on to the Human, or to the Super-Human, on to the Angelic or God-like.

As with the first Great Involution, after vast aeons of time the outward expansion and individualized proliferation of the first Great Evolution reached a point of exhaustion. The centrifugal impulse of the universal-feminine gradually came to a end. It is very important to understand that at the end of the first Great Evolution, the Involuted Word had not completely unfolded itself or entirely regained its lost estate in pure God-consciousness. The increased cosmic will required to manifest a universal profusion of elementary particles rapidly depleted the expanding impulse of the feminine-principle.

5.11   Additional Periods of Involution and Evolution: The Days and Nights of Brahma

After a brief cosmic pause, the next Great Involution began, with one significant difference—all the individualized particles that had been manifested during the first Great Evolution were retained. They were not destroyed or "unmanifested" but were instead compressed along with the entire universe into another condensed cosmic nucleus. Therefore, the second Great Involution was not as deep as the first one; the lowest degree of matter was much higher than before. When the second Great Evolution began, the super-compressed particles acted as the seed-beginnings for the more advanced particles that sprang into manifestation. In this way, the Involuted Word slowly progressed, gradually discarding the lowest veils of matter that stifled the bright light of God-consciousness.

By the end of the second Great Evolution, some of the elementary, subatomic particles were advanced enough in development to constitute the primordial beginning of a "mineral kingdom." These "minerals" were of course much more primitive in arrangement than the magnificent crystalline formations of present-day minerals.

The second Great Evolution was of course followed by a third involutionary period. As experienced by the Logos-

Word, the alternating periods of involution and evolution are cosmically comparable to the human experience of sleeping and waking, of nightime rest and daytime activity. Consequently, in Hindu cosmology these alternating cycles are termed the "Days and Nights of Brahma" (the Universal Creator). As described by H.P. Blavatsky in *The Secret Doctrine* (2011):

> The cycle of creation of the lives of Kosmos is run down; the energy of the manifested "Word" having its growth, culmination, and decrease, as have all things temporal, however long their duration. The Creative Force is eternal as Noumenon [God]; as a phenomenal manifestation, in its aspects, it [the Word] has a beginning and must, therefore, have an end. During that interval, it has its periods of activity and its periods of rest. And these are the Days and Nights of Brahma.

An additional description has been given by Yogi Ramacharaka in *Lessons in Gnani Yoga*:

> The Yogi Teachings contain much regarding the "Days and Nights of Brahm"; the "Inbreathing and Outbreathing of the Creative Principle"; the periods of *"Manvantara,"* and the periods of *"Pralaya."* This thought runs through all the Oriental thought, although in different forms, and with various interpretations. The thought refers to the occult truth that there is in Cosmic Nature alternate periods of Activity and Inactivity—Days and Nights—Inbreathings and Outbreathings—Wakefulness and Sleep. This fundamental law manifests in all Nature, from Universes to Atoms.

Corresponding to the human experience of sleep, then, during a period of involution the Logos-Word ceases all outward activity, and by withdrawing inwardly into nocturnal darkness, outer perception is dimmed into unconsciousness.

Moreover, by inward consolidation the forces of manifestation are strengthened and rejuvenated. Likewise, during a period of evolution the Logos-Word engages in multifarious expansive activity, and by advancing outwardly into the light of day, outer perception is elevated in conscious awareness. Moreover, by outward expression, increasingly advanced forms of life are manifested and further experience is gained.

As in human development, the Primal Logos does not reach full maturity in one single day and night, but by undergoing numerous cosmic Days and Nights, numerous periods of involution and evolution. The current evolutionary period of the universe (which science estimates began about 3.7 billion years ago) has been preceded by numerous cosmic Days and Nights (at least 13 that the author is aware of).

5.12   The Lost Word Begins to Find Itself

By the close of the third evolutionary period, ultra-primitive plant-like forms were developed, along with more advanced minerals and elementary particles. These ancestral plants were of course quite unlike the plant forms of today; nevertheless they were characterized by a more autonomous, indwelling life activity than the mineral forms. The fourth evolutionary period, as one might expect, developed crude animal-like creatures that began to exhibit sensory awareness and primitive feeling. Each evolutionary period retained the forms manifested in the preceding periods, but continued to refine and improve them. By this process, the Logos-Word was able to acquire increased knowledge and experience in an effort to further unfold its God-reflecting nature. This was logically necessary since the Logos-Word is not omniscient, all-knowing, like its divine Creator.

It was only near the end of the fifth evolutionary period

that a crude form was developed in which there were not only the faint stirrings of life and sentience, but more significantly, there was the rudimentary spark of self-awareness. After vast aeons of time and effort, the Lost Word had finally begun to discover itself. To esoteric science, any form—no matter what the shape, conditions or materials—that attains even the faintest glimmer of self-awareness is understood to manifest a "human-like" stage of development. The ultra-primeval forms that constituted the ancestral humans of the fifth evolutionary period would be quite grotesque and unrecognizable today.

Nevertheless, it was by means of these crude life-forms that the Logos-Word achieved a special kind of consciousness that it did not divinely possess at the dawn of its creation—universal self-consciousness. Since divine self-awareness is generated (begotten) by the reciprocating activity of divine expansion (the Holy Mother) and divine contraction (the Heavenly Father), the Logos-Word (as the image of God) can likewise only develop universal self-awareness by the continual cosmic alternations of involution and evolution. Universal self-awareness is not something that can simply be divinely bestowed; it is something that must also be "generated." Moreover, as in human experience, awareness *of* one's "self" can only be achieved *by* oneself; it is not something that someone can do for another. Therefore, the Logos-Word had to come to its own realization of itself. Though God, of course, could assist in providing the necessary circumstances for the Logos-Word to realize itself, it was not logically possible for God to be self-aware for his own creation.

In the case of God, divine self-consciousness is eternally generated; that is, it has always existed—it never had a beginning. In the case of the Logos-Word, however, universal self-consciousness can only occur over time and therefore had a definite beginning in the fifth evolutionary period. Like everything in finite creation, universal self-awareness requires sufficient time to unfold and could not be generated all at once, on its own. As the feminine-principle (the universal-mother) is the cosmic reflection of the Holy Mother, and as the masculine-principle (the universal-father) is the cosmic reflection of the Heavenly Father, so universal self-awareness is the cosmic reflection of the Eternal Son.

In order to acquire universal self-awareness, it was necessary that the Logos-Word turn its attention away from the resplendent light of God at the start of creation and to focus deeply into its own nature. If the Primal Word had been constrained to gaze entirely toward the Son-light of God for all time, every autonomous activity arising from its own nature would have been paralyzed, like a cosmic "deer in the headlights." As the "divine image," the "mirror of God," the Logos-Word would certainly have reflected the light of God, but it would never have been capable of independent self-reflection, of knowing that it was a "living mirror" created by God.

Moreover, for the Logos-Word to differentiate its own radiant nature (at the highest level) from the divine light of spirit infinitely before it, would have been comparable to being able to perceive the faint light of a candle when placed in front of a full summer sun—in other words, impossible to do. Hence the need for the Primal Word to darken its pristine nature, to soot itself with the charcoal of matter. In this way the heavenly-Adam could distinguish his own nature from the light-filled nature of God that surrounded him on all sides.

5.13 The Reason for Individualized Centres of Expression

At this point, two questions naturally arise: (1) "Why didn't the Logos-Word *evolve* its entire nature "as a whole," since it had completely *involved* its entire nature "en masse" in the beginning?" And in this connection, (2) "Why was the Logos-Word impelled by its God-given nature to achieve self-awareness through multiple, individualized life-forms rather than through a single, universal level of vibration?" As we shall see, there are a number of satisfying answers to these greater, cosmic mysteries.

Part of the answer to these mysteries is in recalling the nature of the universal feminine principle which predominates during each evolutionary phase. As a reflection of the Holy Mother, the nature of the universal-feminine is to expand outwardly through the forces of proliferation, propagation, generation, reproduction and multiplication. Not surprisingly, then, multiple centres of individualized activity and expression are continually manifested during each evolutionary period.

A further reason for manifesting multiple centres of activity and expression within the Logos-Word is to gain increased experience and knowledge. By manifesting multiform microcosmic replicas of itself at various levels of development, the universal nature of the Logos-Word is expanded in rich complexity, wondrous detail and heterogeneous interaction. As the unitary lustre of an uncut diamond is given amplified brilliance by dividing the surface into numerous, small facets, the Universal Word more brilliantly reflects the light of God by manifesting innumerable facets of itself.

Moreover, by manifesting life-forms that are sentient, conscious, self-aware and capable of reflecting the light of God, the Universal Word generates other finite beings, other finite persons that mirror the reality of God. As explained by Yogi Ramacharaka:

[T]he whole effort of the Divine Will seems to be in the direction of "raising up" Individual Egos to higher and still higher forms. And in order to produce such Egos the process of "Involution" of Principles seems to have been caused, and the subsequent wonderful Evolutionary process instituted ... And the work was always in the direction of causing higher and higher "forms" to arise—higher and higher Units—higher and higher Centers. But in every form, center or unit, there was manifested the Three Principles, Mind, Energy, and Matter. And within each was the ever present Spirit. For Spirit must be in All—just as All must be in Spirit ...

And, so this Evolutionary process has continued ever since, and must continue for aeons yet. The Absolute [through the Logos-Word] is raising itself up into Itself higher and higher sheaths in which to manifest ... And the whole end and aim of it all seems to be that Egos may reach the stage where they are conscious of the Real Self—of the Spirit within them, and its relation to the Spirit of the Absolute ... (*Lessons in Gnani Yoga*; 1934)

Once again, by generating independent beings within itself, the life experience of the Universal Word is abundantly magnified.

But aside from the advantages for the Universal Word of generating a countless array of independent beings, there is also an incomparable, benevolent benefit for these "children of the Word"—the gift of life! By having an enduring existence within the Universal Word, these microcosmic entities can also experience the light of God reflected within their differentiated finite natures, and thereby also unite themselves to the spirit of love. In other words, the cosmic impulse to generate new life-centres directly springs from the loving action of spirit which eternally begets the life of the Eternal Son. As the image of God, the Logos-Word is therefore divinely compelled to likewise generate independent life from its own nature with no thought of advantage or reward for itself.

But perhaps the deepest and primary reason for the cosmic evolutionary impulse to individualize is for the created Word to experience a glimmer of the infinite joy of the Trinity. Since this infinite joy is eternally engendered by the loving relationship of three divine persons, in order for the Logos-Word to experience something similar, there needs to be other "persons" in creation similar to itself. Though the Logos-Word, as a universal person, certainly has a relationship to the divine persons of the Trinitarian God, it is obviously not a co-equal relationship. It is impossible for the Logos-Word to enter fully into the lives of the infinite and eternal persons of God. But, by differentiating other life-forms within its nature that possess independent personhood, the Logos-Word can "share itself" with other similar persons. Through differentiation, then, the Macrocosmic-Adam is not alone; he has companionship and the joy of sharing love with other persons. Likewise, the self-conscious life-forms (persons) individualized by the Logos-Word are given the same opportunity for companionship and love.

CHAPTER 6

THE ONE LIFE BECOMES MANY:
THE COSMIC HIERARCHY OF BEINGS

6.1 The Riddle of the One and the Many

EVEN THOUGH the cosmic process of evolving individualized centers of self-awareness (persons) is an observable fact on earth, it is still conceptually difficult to visualize exactly how the one universal life of the Logos-Word becomes many individualized lives in creation and still remains one universal life. Throughout esoteric history, this conceptual paradox has been known as the "Riddle of the One and the Many." As described in *The Secret Doctrine of the Rosicrucians*:

> [T]he Rosicrucian is directed to apply his attention to the concept of the World Soul [Logos-Word]—the First Manifestation of the Eternal Parent—as a One manifesting as Many; a Unity manifesting as Diversity; an Identical manifesting as Variety: yet, notwithstanding such manifestations, remaining ever One, Unity, and Identical ... That all beings are, in truth, but expressions

of the One [Universal] Being—centres of consciousness, form, and activity within itself—is a fundamental tenet of all occult and esoteric teachings of the past and present, occidental and oriental, philosophical and theological. (Magus Incognito. 1949)

As often the case when mentally grappling with the greater mysteries, understanding can be gained by applying the Hermetic law of correspondence: "As above, so below; as below, so above." In this instance, a familiar scene in Nature can be used as a helpful analogy. Visualize a small, tranquil pond on a bright sunny day. On the smooth surface of the pond, there is a single, glorious reflection of the sun in the sky. A strong wind suddenly picks up and causes numerous waves to occur on the surface of the pond. The large, single refection of the sun is no longer observed, but instead a dazzling array of tiny solar reflections dancing across the waves.

The tranquil pond in this analogy represents the reflective nature of the Logos-Word. The sun in the sky naturally represents God. As the tranquil pond mirrors the sun in the sky, the Logos-Word mirrors the light of God. But when the surface of the pond was stirred up by the wind, the single, unitary reflection of the sun was multiplied into numerous points of light—a sparking profusion of miniature suns occurred. Similar to the strong wind, when the feminine principle of the Logos-Word generated numerous independent waves (that is, vibrational centres) in the universal nature of the Logos-Word, multiple reflections of God (that is, self-conscious life-forms: persons) appeared.

Continuing the analogy, even though the rippled surface of the pond no longer reflected a large, single image of the sun, it still reflected the sun—but as a multitude of miniature suns. Moreover, whether tranquil or rippled, the pond remains a pond, and the reflective nature of water is unchanged. Similarly, even though the differentiated nature of the Logos-Word no longer reflects a universal image of God, it still reflects the light of God—but in multitude, self-conscious life-forms. Moreover, whether its nature is uniform or diversified, the Logos-Word remains the one universal life, and it continues to be the one universal mirror of God.

6.2 Reflecting the One Life of God

When considering the profusion of life-forms that have been gradually evolved, it is important to understand that the Logos-Word does *not* have the capacity to *create* life; it can only differentiate the substance of its own universal life. There is, of course, only one life—the life of God. As the divine self-concept created by God, the Logos-Word does not logically "self-exist" as does the divine Creator. Only God is infinitely and eternally alive in himself; the Logos-Word is therefore completely dependent on God for its life. Moreover, since the Logos-Word is a divine creation, its life has a birth and a boundary; it is temporal and finite. The Logos-Word, then, has a diminished and contingent form of divine life; what is esoterically termed, "universal life." Once again, only God possesses infinite and eternal life.

Though finite and temporal in nature, compared to all other life-forms in the universe, the Logos-Word exhibits a supernal degree of life. This is due to a fundamental axiom of Nature: "The degree of life that a created form exhibits is in direct proportion to the degree that it reflects the divine light, the living reality of God, in itself." A plant form, therefore, exhibits a greater degree of life than a mineral form because the higher vibrational nature of the plant reflects a greater degree of divine life. The human form displays a higher level of consciousness and being than does an animal form because the higher vibrational nature of the human reflects a greater degree of divine life. Furthermore, there are numerous other life-forms in cosmic existence today that are far more advanced than human forms and which, therefore, exhibit a far greater degree of life, consciousness and being. Though these superhuman life-forms (such as angels and archangels) are not yet recognized by physical science, many are quite familiar to religious study and to esoteric investigation.

Since the Logos-Word has undergone numerous Days and Nights of cosmic evolution and involution, the life-forms in the universe today are considerably more advanced than the primeval, elemental forms of the early phases of unfoldment. Presently, the universe is enormously complex and extensively populated with resplendent beings of high advancement. Correspondingly, the overall vibrational level of the Logos-Word has been significantly raised. Many of the densest levels of matter, energy and mind are no longer in existence. The overall mirroring capacity of the Word is far less darkened and opaque. In consequence, the Logos-Word is now unimaginably self-aware, self-enlightened and much nearer to the level of God-consciousness that it innately reflected in the beginning.

As the Logos-Word has grown and matured as the "universal person," it now experiences a far greater degree of free-will. Initially, the Primal Word was involuntarily compelled by its God-given nature to act in specific ways. As it continued to vibrationally rise up from the unconscious levels of dense matter, the Primal Word became increasingly aware of, understood, and willingly acceded to the wise direction of its own God-reflective nature. In the early cycles of cosmic evolution, individualized forms were developed primarily by trial-and-error. As universal development advanced, life-forms and life-activity were increasingly directed by the wise and loving will of the Logos-Word acting in free communion with divine inspiration.

6.3   Life-Forms as the Thoughts of the Logos-Word

Fundamental to answering the "Riddle of the One and the Many" is the knowledge that the absolute, infinite mind possesses the innate capacity to create a living idea of itself. Not surprisingly, a similar capacity has been inherited by the Logos-Word; that is, the innate ability to generate thoughts and ideas out of its own mental nature. While any thought or idea of the Logos-Word is obviously not as real and alive as is a divine idea, a universal idea can nevertheless endure for vast aeons of cosmic time.

The primordial elementary particles that were spontaneously propagated at the dawn of the first Great Evolution are correctly understood to be the crude, elementary ideas of the new-born Word. Furthermore, these miniscule ideas were multiple mental replicas of the original Primal Atom; that is, the Logos-Word in a one-dimensional state of supercompression into matter. In other words, these basic elementary ideas were multiple copies of the first, crude self-concept generated by the Primal Word. Just as the first idea conceived in the mind of God is the divine self-concept, the first idea conceived (in multiple form) by the Logos-Word is its own self-concept. However, unlike the perfect self-concept generated in the divine mind, the first self-concept generated by the unconscious, materially-darkened Word was crude and imperfect.

Continuing this line of understanding, all the increasingly developed life-forms that were evolved in subsequent cosmic Days by the Logos-Word were essentially improved self-concepts; that is, more advanced ideas about what and who the Logos-Being thought it was. And of course, due to the propagating activity of the universal feminine-principle, any new idea of the Logos-Word was prolifically multiplied. What should also be recognized in this connection is a further fundamental axiom of "Nature" (that is, the nature of the

Logos-Word): "All advanced life-forms must recapitulate (in microcosmic form) all earlier macrocosmic stages of development." This natural axiom explains why all advanced life-forms undergo a gradual process of growth and development. As one particular example, the human form must therefore microcosmically recapitulate the mineral, plant and animal stages of cosmic evolution before it can undergo specific human development.

6.4 Advanced Ideas of the Logos-Word as Independent Persons

As the evolving Logos-Word increased in self-awareness and better understood itself as a cosmic being, as a universal person divinely gifted with life, consciousness, free-will and immortal existence, the associated self-concepts that were generated reflected these advancements. Therefore, even though all life-forms are ideas in the mental nature of the Logos-Word, advanced life-forms (as advanced cosmic self-concepts) are characterized by independent personhood; they are not simply will-less, servile extensions of the Logos-Word.

Even though advanced life-forms possess independent personhood, they are obviously not equal in stature and attainment to the person of the Word. Nevertheless, they do share in the reflective mental nature of the Logos-Word, and are equal persons in that respect. The Logos-Word can therefore be regarded as the "senior person" to all the "junior persons" generated as universal self-concepts. Or in more familial terms, the Logos-Word can be considered the loving, macrocosmic parent to all the microcosmic children conceived in the womb of Nature.

Possessing self-awareness, advanced life-forms, like their cosmic parent, are able to generate their own self-concepts, to mentally declare, "I am." When God declares, "I AM," a living, universal being is created in the absolute, infinite mind. When the Logos-Word declares, "I am," independent life-forms are manifested within its universal mental nature. When less advanced life-forms (such as human beings) correspondingly declare, "I am," these self-concepts exist simply as ephemeral thoughts within the confines of their own personal minds—they do not have any independent life of their own. However, when more highly developed life-forms (such as cherubim and seraphim) declare "I am," or mentally formulate similar thoughts, these also become independent life-forms in universal Nature.

Evolutionary development as it occurs in the universe today, therefore, is very much a shared activity of numerous life-forms. Highly advanced beings now work cooperatively with the Logos-Word for mutual development, for the benefit of simpler life-forms and to raise the general vibratory level of the entire universe. Since the cosmos now embodies the accumulated wisdom of numerous Days and Nights of development, the universal nature of the Logos-Word is now highly organized, as is the complex interaction of all the advanced beings within it.

6.5 The Universal Hierarchy of Advanced Being

Western theology,[15] certain Greek and Hebrew traditions[16] and anthroposophical spiritual science all recognize nine distinct levels of superphysical existence above humanity (not including the Logos-Word and the Triune God). Since "advanced beings" are here defined as all life-forms that possess self-awareness, human beings have also been included as a tenth cosmic level of advanced existence (see Figure 9 below). Except for the composite Hebrew tradition cited here, the other ideological systems also arrange the nine levels into three equal major divisions: the First Hierarchy, the Second Hierarchy and the Third Hierarchy.[17]

	WESTERN THEOLOGY	HEBREW TRADITION	GREEK TRADITION	ANTHROPOSOPHY
THE TRIUNE GOD	THE BLESSED TRINITY (INCLUDES)	YAHWEH	THEOS	THE TRINITY
THE WORD	THE WORD	MEMRA	LOGOS	THE CREATIVE WORD
FIRST HIERARCHY	SERAPHIM	CHAIOTH HA-QADESH	(SERAPHIM)	SPIRITS OF LOVE
FIRST HIERARCHY	CHERUBIM	AUPHANIM	(CHERUBIM)	SPIRITS OF HARMONY
FIRST HIERARCHY	THRONES	CHASHMALIM	(THRONES)	SPIRITS OF WILL
SECOND HIERARCHY	DOMINIONS	SERAPHIM	KYRIOTETES	SPIRITS OF WISDOM
SECOND HIERARCHY	VIRTUES	MALACHIM	DYNAMEIS	SPIRITS OF MOVEMENT
SECOND HIERARCHY	POWERS	ELOHIM	EXUSIAI	SPIRITS OF FORM
THIRD HIERARCHY	PRINCIPALITIES	BENE ELOHIM	ARCHAI	TIME SPIRITS
THIRD HIERARCHY	ARCHANGELS	KERUBIM	ARCHANGELOI	SUN SPIRITS
THIRD HIERARCHY	ANGELS	ISHIM	ANGELOI	MOON SPIRITS
	HUMANITY	BENEI-ADAM	ANTHROPOS	SPIRITS OF FREEDOM

Figure 9: The Universal Hierarchy of Being

The various levels have been classified vertically based on the nearness each advanced being is to God in conscious existence and attainment. Furthermore, except for humans, all other beings inhabit life-forms that transcend physical matter and are, therefore, invisible to ordinary perception. Moreover, the higher the level of advancement, the larger the sphere of influence and activity—extending from planetary, to galactic, to cosmic. While human activity is basically confined to the earth, for instance, the conscious activity of the cherubim and seraphim encompasses the entire Milky Way galaxy. The preceding chart, entitled "The Universal Hierarchy of Beings," should prove helpful in conceptually organizing these diverse, advanced beings.

The various levels of being are not arbitrary, but reflect a significant degree of advancement toward full God-consciousness that a lower level does not, as yet, possess. Not surprisingly, then, the higher the level of attainment, the longer the evolutionary time that was required to achieve it. In general, then, more advanced beings have been in existence longer than less advanced life-forms. In fact, some highly exalted beings (such as those of the first hierarchy) came into existence during a previous evolutionary Day of manifestation, whereas present-day humanity came into existence during the current evolutionary Day.

It should also be understood that arranging the various levels of universal being as illustrated in Figure 9 does not mean that all these advanced life-forms are similarly stacked up on each other like some enormous "cosmic layer cake." Many of these life-forms vibrationally interpenetrate each other and the same cosmic space, similar to the interaction of various energy vibrations. The space in a typical home, for example, can be permeated with heat energy, light energy, gravitational energy, magnetic energy, ultra-violet energy, sound energy, electrical energy and numerous radio waves. While all these forms of energy can occupy the same space at the same time, they don't necessary affect one another due to their differences in vibration. Within the same cosmic space, then, numerous angels, archangels and principalities may be independently active without necessarily perceiving or affecting one another.

Since evolutionary progress is logically ever-upward, humans today will in time attain an angel-like level of development, then an archangel-like level and so on. These future levels of attainment for humanity will also be in advance of today's higher levels. In other words, humanity's angel-like stage of evolution will be more advanced than the present-day angels. Likewise, the future human stage for the current animal kingdom will be superior to today's human beings. Cosmic evolution, then, is an ever-ascending spiral of advancement with each higher level unfolding increased life, consciousness and being. In this way, individual life-forms are perfected, which in turn contributes to the total enrichment of the Logos-Word; a good example of the saying: "As the rose adorns itself, it adorns the entire garden."

6.6 The Three Great Realms of Cosmic Existence

Planet earth is not just the exclusive domain of human beings; it is the life-sustaining location for certain plants and animals as well. Moreover, the mineral kingdom not only constitutes the physical foundation of the earth, but it is spread throughout the material universe. All life-forms that incorporate dense, sense-perceptible matter in some way belong to what is commonly known as the "physical world." To empirical science, the physical realm is the only certainty that exists in the universe. To esoteric wisdom, however, the entire universe is differentiated into three great realms, or worlds, of cosmic existence, only one of which is the physical world.[18] The other two realms are esoterically termed the "celestial world" and the "soul world." These two realms are not characterized by the dense materiality of the physical world, and are therefore imperceptible to the physical senses. Nevertheless, like many invisible energies and beings in the universe, the celestial world and the soul world can be known through their effects in the physical world (as well as by supersensible perception, of course).

Though each of these realms is qualitatively distinct from the others, they are all universal and interpenetrate one another vibrationally. Each of these universal realms is characterized by the vibrational degree of matter, energy and mind that composes it. The physical world is composed of the densest forms of matter, energy and mind. The soul world is composed of higher degrees of matter, energy and mind that are not found in the physical world. The celestial world (also esoterically referred to as "spirit-land") is composed of the finest degrees of matter, energy and mind as yet unfolded in the universe. Not surprisingly, the celestial world is the universal abode of the most highly advanced beings in cosmic evolution; while the soul world is home to less advanced beings; and the physical world is inhabited by the least developed life-forms in evolution.

Each of the three cosmic realms of existence is further subdivided into seven major regions, for a total of 21 cosmic regions of existence (see Figure 10 below). Once again, these divisions are not arbitrary or invented. Analogous to the seven distinct colours of the visible light spectrum (red, orange, yellow, green, blue, indigo and violet), each of these seven cosmic regions is qualitatively different from the others, and not just a refinement or densification of vibration. The colour red, for instance, is qualitatively different than the colour yellow, even though they are both vibrations of light. Similarly in the physical world, solid matter is qualitatively different than liquid matter, even though they are both vibrational degrees of matter.

Based on these qualitative differences, the seven subdivisions in each of the cosmic realms of existence are

further separated into two broad categories: a higher and a
lower section, esoterically referred to as "planes." There are,
therefore, six cosmic planes of existence within the three
cosmic realms.

THE COSMIC REALMS OF EXISTENCE	THE COSMIC PLANES OF EXISTENCE	THE COSMIC REGIONS OF EXISTENCE
CELESTIAL WORLD (SPIRIT LAND)	HIGHER HEAVENLY PLANE	7. GERMINAL IDEAS OF FORM
		6. GERMINAL IDEAS OF LIFE
		5. GERMINAL IDEAS OF SOUL
	LOWER HEAVENLY PLANE	4. ARCHETYPES OF INTEGRATION
		3. ARCHETYPES OF SOUL
		2. ARCHETYPES OF LIFE
		1. ARCHETYPES OF FORM
SOUL WORLD	UPPER ASTRAL PLANE	7. SOUL LIFE
		6. ACTIVE SOUL FORCE
		5. SOUL LIGHT
	LOWER ASTRAL PLANE	4. LIKING AND DISLIKING
		3. WISHES
		2. MOBILE SENSITIVITY
		1. BURNING DESIRE
PHYSICAL WORLD	ETHERIC PLANE	7. LIFE ETHER
		6. TONE (CHEMICAL) ETHER
		5. LIGHT ETHER
		4. WARMTH ETHER
	MATERIAL PLANE	3. GASEOUS MATTER
		2. LIQUID MATTER
		1. SOLID MATTER

Figure 10: The Cosmic Realms, Planes and Regions of Existence

6.7 The Physical Realm of Cosmic Existence

The lower subdivision of the physical world—the material
plane—is the one that is most familiar to empirical science

and also to most human beings. The three cosmic regions of solid, liquid and gaseous matter are all perceptible to the five physical senses of sight, sound, smell, taste and touch. We know from sensory observation that the three material regions together exist in a wide variety of combinations throughout the universe. On earth, for example, solid, liquid and gaseous matter are all diffused throughout the planet; but not everywhere, evenly or equally. Most of the solid matter is gathered together in the lithosphere, most of the liquid matter is gathered together in the hydrosphere, and most of the gaseous matter is gathered together in the atmosphere.

The higher subdivision of the physical world—the etheric plane—is as yet unrecognized by empirical science and by most human beings. This is because the four cosmic regions of warmth ether, light ether, tone (or chemical) ether and life ether are not perceptible to the physical senses, though they are perceptible to the superphysical senses. While the four etheric regions are invisible to ordinary perception, most of what we describe today as "energy": heat, light, magnetism, electricity and gravity are, in fact, etheric effects.

As ultra-rarified physical material, each ether serves as an intermediary between the universal manifestations of matter and energy, thereby conveying the higher vibrational actions of certain forces into the physical world. The current esoteric understanding of ether is, however, far different from the ancient Greek concept of "aether" and also quite different from the nineteenth-century scientific notion of the "luminiferous ether." In Greek mythology, aether was the super-fine substance that filled the starry dome of heaven above the earth. As humans breathed air, the Greek gods inhaled aether. Aristotle also included aether as the fifth classical element (the "quintessence") above earth, water, air and fire.

In the case of luminiferous ether, this was briefly hypothesized by science to explain the observation that light (and all electromagnetic radiation) can travel in waves. The luminiferous (or "light") ether, then, was believed to be the invisible medium that propagated waves of light. Early theorists, however, mistakenly attributed mechanical properties to the luminiferous ether, such as fluidity, rigidity, elasticity and internal friction. The well-known Michelson-Morley experiment in 1887 demonstrated that such a tensile medium did not exist. Noted physicist, Albert Einstein, later replaced the luminiferous ether with the ingenious concept of "physical space."[19] Einsteinian space is not the "absolute emptiness" of Newtonian physics. While it is regarded as a universal medium lacking the mechanical properties of the luminiferous ether, Einsteinian space has been demonstrated to possess certain morphological properties; for example, it can be curved and bent. As explained by Russian-born physicist and cosmologist, George Gamow (1904–1968):

> Light ether is a substance of a peculiar type, which has no similarity to the familiar atomic-mosaic that we usually call matter. We can call light ether a "substance" (if only because it serves as a grammatical subject for the verb "to vibrate"), but we can also call it "space," keeping in mind that ... space may possess certain morphological or structural features that make it a much more complicated thing than it is in the conceptions of Euclidian geometry. In fact, in modern physics the expressions "light ether" (divested of its alleged mechanical properties) and "physical space" are considered synonymous. (*One Two Three ... Infinity*; 1988)

In other words, according to modern physics, light ether is not a medium that fills empty space, it *is* cosmic space. Instead of saying that light energy travels as waves through the light ether, it is now more scientifically common to say that light waves are propagated through the medium of space.

To esoteric science, however, supersensible ether is a

much more complicated aspect of the physical world than is Einsteinian space. As already mentioned, clairvoyant perception distinguishes four separate and unique etheric regions, whereas modern physics recognizes only one universal condition of space. Moreover, at a certain level of vibration, ether is supersensibly perceived to be "emptier than space," more akin to the scientific notion of "black holes."[20] As explained by spiritual scientist, Rudolf Steiner:

> [I]n the transition from quantifiable matter to ether, rarefaction plays no part ... not only does matter become empty space, but it becomes negative, *less* than nothing—emptier than emptiness; it assumes a 'sucking' nature. Ether is sucking, absorbing. Matter *presses*, ether *absorbs*. (*Mystery of the Universe: The Human Being, Image of Creation*; 1920)

This quality of being "negative space" makes each of the four etheric regions an excellent medium for the transmission of numerous subtle forces and energies, particularly those necessary for physical life on earth. The lowest cosmic region, esoterically termed the "warmth" or "fire" ether, transmits supersensible forces that establish internal warmth and regulate body temperature in living forms. The region of "light ether" transmits supersensible forces that endow living forms with an internal, vital luminosity that directs and shapes important organic activity. The primary source of light ether within our own planetary system is, not surprisingly, the sun.

The third gradation of macrocosmic ether has been given a variety of terms due to its unique formative activities. For instance, it has been termed the "chemical ether" since it transmits supersensible forces that organize material existence according to number and weight. Moreover, by means of this etheric level, forces are active within living forms that are similar to chemical attraction and repulsion, but which instead actuate the metabolic processes of nutrition and elimination. The mathematically organizing forces of this particular etheric level are clairaudiently perceived as supersensible sound, which accounts for the alternate terms of "sound ether" and "tone ether." The fourth and highest cosmic region of ether is termed the "life ether," and is characterized by supersensible forces that establish replication and reproduction in living forms.

In general, then, the four regions of the etheric plane convey the supersensible vital forces and organic rhythms of Nature that are crucially necessary for physical life. Not surprisingly, then, responsible esotericists are very cautious about revealing specific details of the etheric plane since misapplication and misuse of life-sustaining etheric forces would have disastrous physical consequences.

Similar to the cosmic regions of solid, liquid and gaseous matter, the four etheric regions are not separately layered on top of each other, parfait-style, throughout the cosmos. They are interwoven with each other and with the three universal regions of the material plane in a complicated tapestry of formations. As well as being entwined in a myriad of homogenous combinations, each etheric region is known to gather in vast, uneven concentrations analogous to the countless planetary and stellar lithospheres, hydrospheres and atmospheres of the universal material plane.

6.8 The Soul Realm of Cosmic Existence

If esoteric information concerning the etheric plane of the physical world appears outlandish to modern science, no doubt supersensible research concerning the next highest level of cosmic existence—the soul world—is empirically regarded as the product of wild hallucination or even insanity. In the mundane eyes of modern science, feelings and emotions are generally regarded as the cerebral effects of chemical occurrences within the physical body and, therefore, do not exist apart from organic activity. To the esoteric researcher, however, even though there is an obvious psychosomatic connection between body chemistry and emotion—passions, feelings, desires and emotions are perceived to have independent existence apart from organic chemistry, and to have their origin and essentiality in the astral substances and forces of the macrocosmic soul world.

Strange as it may seem to the materialistically minded of today, those fleeting and ephemeral feelings that mysteriously appear and disappear within our consciousness actually have their origin, not in the physical world, but in a higher realm of soul substance and energy. As with the macrocosmic physical world, supersensible perception distinguishes seven major regions to the soul world, four of which are associated with the lower astral plane, and three of which are associated with the higher astral plane (see Figure 10).

The distinguishing characteristic of astral substance in all regions of the soul world is incessant vibratory motion and activity; so much so, that astral substance can accurately be described as "living force-material." Moreover, in spite of their particularity, all soul regions are determined and governed by the interaction of two fundamental soul forces: "sympathy" and "antipathy." Sympathy, as esoterically defined, is the centripetal soul force that naturally draws astral substance and energy together. Antipathy, on the other hand, is the centrifugal soul force that distances astral substance and energy from each other. The fluctuating tension between sympathy and antipathy in the soul world is, of course, the diminished astral echo of the divine interaction of the Heavenly Father and the Holy Mother.

The lowest cosmic region of the soul world, as termed in modern-day spiritual science (anthroposophy), is the "region of burning desire." Not surprisingly, this is the source and abode of all coarse passion and primitive desire. Like all regions in all three worlds, the region of burning desire can be further subdivided into finer distinctions, in this case ranging from primeval, magmatic lustfulness to smoldering, all-consuming ravenousness. In this region of the lower astral plane, the soul force of antipathy overwhelmingly dominates all forces, substances and formations. What little sympathetic soul force is active, takes on the character of selfish, insatiable greed. Since the soul formations in this lower region repel much of the surrounding astral environment, they whirl through soul space resistant to change and, therefore, analogously correspond to the solid, lithospheric formations of the physical world (such as earthly continents).

The next highest region of the lower astral plane, termed the "region of mobile sensitivity," is characterized by an equal balance of sympathetic soul forces and antipathetic soul forces. Consequently, astral formations on this level react neutrally to much of the surrounding soul environment and can, therefore, be analogously compared to the fluid nature of a hydrosphere in the physical world (such as earthly oceans). In human experience, the neutral psychological reaction to certain sensory impressions can be traced to the astral forces and substances of this particular soul region.

In the soul region vibrationally above mobile sensitivity, the soul force of sympathy becomes the predominating impulse. As a result, the forces, substances and formations of the cosmic "region of wishes" reach out in all directions in their astral environment and are thereby compared to the expanding, gaseous formations of the physical world (such as the earthly atmosphere). Nevertheless, the soul force of antipathy is still strongly present and this tinges the all-embracing sympathetic forces in this region with a grey hue of selfishness.

The highest gradation of the lower astral plane, the "region of liking and disliking," functions as an intermediary borderland between the lower astral and the higher astral regions. The dominating soul force of sympathy results in a pervasive, permeating diffusion of "liking" throughout soul space that is comparable to the interpenetration of warmth energy in the physical world. As cold is simply a lessening of heat, "disliking" in the soul world is simply a diminution of liking.

The three soul regions of the upper astral plane, because of the predominant, all-embracing power of sympathy, are characterized by a bright, unifying activity that radiates outwardly to illuminate and suffuse the discordant, antipathetic formations of the lower astral plane. Not surprisingly, then, the first upper region is termed the "region of soul light" and corresponds to the all-encompassing action of sunlight in the physical world. The two highest regions of the soul world, the "region of active soul force" and the "region of soul life," are both characterized by an even deeper sympathetic penetration and a much more extensive power of unification throughout the entire soul world.

6.9   The Celestial Realm of Cosmic Existence

As the great soul world is the cosmic source of all the affective force-material that manifests as human emotion and feeling, the great celestial world is the realm of cosmic existence from which is drawn all the numinous stuff of human thought. Today, however, most human thought activity is only a pale, shadow reflection of the living, macrocosmic ideation that pervades the entire created universe. In anthroposophy, the celestial world is also termed, "spirit-land," which is equally applicable as long as it is understood that this cosmic realm is not *comprised of* spirit substance but is the realm *closest to* the spirit reality of God. As such, the vibratory material of the celestial world is "spirit-like" in nature, since only the transcendent essentiality of God is truly "spirit."

As with the two lower realms of cosmic existence, the celestial world is divisible into seven cosmic regions: four regions comprise the "lower heavenly plane" and three regions comprise the "higher heavenly plane." This sevenfold division has been traditionally recognized in Judaism, Christianity and Islam as the "seven heavens," with the "seventh heaven" being regarded as the highest region of cosmic existence and the abode of highly-perfected, godlike beings.

The four regions of the lower heavenly plane are characterized by vibrantly-mobile, creative mental formations—living ideas, called "archetypes," that shape and determine the diverse manifestations of the two lower worlds. These living archetypes are supersensibly perceived as coruscating thought-formations of colour and sound whose harmonious interaction is esoterically termed, "the music of the spheres." As described by Rudolf Steiner:

> The [supersensible] observer feels as if he were in an ocean of tones, and in these tones, in this spiritual chiming, the beings of the spirit world express themselves. The primordial laws of their existence, their mutual relationships and affinities, express themselves in the intermingling of these sounds, in their harmonies, melodies and rhythms. What the intellect perceives in the physical world as law, as idea, reveals itself to the spiritual ear as spiritual music. Hence, the Pythagoreans called this perception of the spiritual world the "music of the spheres." (*Theosophy*, 1994)

Within the lowest region of the celestial world are found the shape-inducing archetypes that materially manifest in the physical world as mineral, plant, animal and human life-forms. Though these living archetypes are in constant creative motion and activity, the cosmic region itself has a certain enduring quality as compared with the increasingly accelerated regions vibrationally above it. As such, the "region of the archetypes of form" provides the basic, foundational support of the celestial world analogous to the solid, lithospheric formations of the physical world.

The second region of the lower heavenly plane, the "region of the archetypes of life," is characterized by thought-formations that rhythmically interpenetrate and unify the various archetypes of form, analogous to the flowing, liquid hydrospheric formations of the physical world. This harmonious ocean of life-shaping archetypes can also be accurately compared to the rhythmic circulation of vital fluid—blood—in a living organism.

The formative "archetypes of soul" that underlie the feelings and sensations, the joys and sorrows, of all sentient beings existing within the physical and soul worlds have their abode in the third region of the celestial world. Due to the increasingly rarified thought-substance of these cosmic archetypes, this region can be analogously compared to the aeriform domains of the physical world. As well, various emotional expressions generated by beings existing within the two lower worlds have a reciprocating, atmospheric-like effect in this celestial region. A powerful outburst of human anger, for example, is supersensibly perceived to cause a turbulent, celestial tempest. A wistful, human longing is likewise perceived to generate a gentle, celestial breeze. The cumulative passions of a raging battle on earth result in a furious thunderstorm of celestial activity.

The living thought-forms of the fourth, middle region of the celestial world, the "region of archetypes of order and integration," perform a more comprehensive, all-embracing, harmonious directive activity of all the subordinate archetypes of the three, lower celestial regions.

The three highest regions of the celestial world contain the sublime creative forces that are embodied in the various cosmic archetypes of the lower heavenly plane—the "germinal ideas of form," the "germinal ideas of life" and the "germinal ideas of soul." When projected into the lower regions of the celestial world, these living, germinal, ideas effloresce into a myriad of cosmic thought-forms. On the higher heavenly plane, thought substance is imbued with increased supernal meaning and purpose, such that the supersensible tones of celestial music generated on the lower heavenly plane are transformed into cosmic "language." As described by Rudolf Steiner in *Theosophy* (1994):

> The observer with the spiritual ear who rises from the lower regions of spiritland to these higher ranges becomes aware that sounds and tones are transformed into a spiritual language. He begins to perceive the Spiritual Word through which the things and beings no longer make known to him their nature in music alone, but now express it in words. They utter what can be called in spiritual science their *eternal names*.

CHAPTER 7

THE PRIMORDIAL STAGES OF THE EARTH AND SOLAR SYSTEM

7.1 The Cosmic Evolution of Our Solar System

LITTLE IS KNOWN in modern cosmogony about the formation and evolution of our own solar system. The most widely accepted theory today is known as the "nebular hypothesis." This theory proposes that our solar system began as a "pre-solar nebula"—a smaller, condensed core fragment of a vast molecular cloud in space. As the pre-solar nebula continued to collapse under the strength of gravity, it began to form a hot, hydrostatic centre. As the slow, gaseous rotation and collapse increased, the pre-solar nebula flattened into a protoplanetary disk with a dense, powerful, superhot core—a protostar—at the centre. The protostar increased in mass to become the sun, while the protoplanetary disk continued to rotate and selectively condense to form the various planets.

All this scientific conjecture sounds reasonable enough and, in fact, is somewhat supported by esoteric investigation. This shouldn't be too surprising since the basic nebular hypothesis was first proposed in 1734 by Emanuel Swedenborg (1688–1772), a well-known Christian mystic. Esoteric cosmogony concurs with scientific theory that the formation and evolution of our solar system was a lengthy and complex process that occurred in identifiable stages. Moreover, the overall physical, evolutionary events, as scientifically hypothesized, are similarly envisioned in esoteric science; but with one very important difference.[21] From an esoteric perspective, what occurred in the formation and evolution of our solar system was not the result of blind, purposeless forces such as heat and gravity; or lifeless, mechanical movement such as rotational momentum. Consistent with all that has been esoterically said so far concerning the universe, our solar system was, and is, the conscious, intelligent and deliberate design of countless advanced beings. Furthermore, not all of these advanced beings conform or agree with each other. Our solar system, as it is constituted today, is the arena and effect of powerful supersensible cooperation *and* conflict.

7.2 The Four Developmental Stages of the Earth and the Solar System

Theosophical and anthroposophical literature contain a wealth of complex and detailed esoteric information on the formation and evolution of our solar system. Some of this information has been gathered from ancient writings, but most has been acquired from clairvoyantly investigating the "akashic records." Similar to the manner in which impressions, thoughts, feelings and events can be stored as memories in human minds in order to be recalled later, the universal mind of the Logos-Word is capable of retaining the subtlest details of cosmic activity for vast aeons of time. With sufficient initiatory training, this "cosmic memory" is accessible to supersensible investigation. The more highly developed the clairvoyant ability, the further back in cosmic time an esoteric investigator can travel. Needless to say, the primeval cosmic beginnings of our solar system are perceptible to only the highest initiates. What follows is an exceedingly abbreviated summary of the initiate information available.

To begin, it is important to understand that the 4.6 billion year formation of our solar system, as detailed by the nebular hypothesis of modern cosmogony, is according to esoteric research only one developmental stage in a vastly longer evolutionary process. To supersensible investigation, there have been three other developmental stages, equally long or longer, than the present one. Moreover, much of what has occurred during the current evolutionary stage of the solar system is regarded as a concentrated, refined recapitulation of the three previous stages. Therefore, in order to esoterically understand the formational process of our current stage, it makes logical sense to examine the previous stages on which our current solar system is based.

7.3   The First Stage: The "Ancient Saturn Period"

Far, far back in time, but still during the current, cosmic Day of evolution, our solar system began as a vast, nebular sphere of "warmth" in empty space. This was not a protoplanetary body of sense-perceptible heat generated by the friction of gravitationally collapsing interstellar dust (as envisioned by the nebular hypothesis); but was instead a superphysical sphere of warmth ether brought into existence by the advanced beings currently known as the "spirits of will (thrones)." At that time, the spirits of will sacrificially bestowed part of their own etheric warmth in order to provide an arena of activity for other developing beings.

Without going into great detail here, most of the elementary life-forms and advanced beings then in existence were active mostly in the soul and spirit regions surrounded the primeval sphere. Nevertheless, a rudimentary, ephemeral life-form composed entirely of warmth ether slowly came into being within the confines of the etheric sphere, particularly through the delineating efforts of those elevated entities known today as the "spirits of form (powers)."

Though the nebular sphere itself exhibited no permanently-infused life, evanescent currents and mobile configurations within the etheric warmth were the living effects of the various encircling entities. While the rudimentary life-forms were active and differentiated within the substance of the sphere, the overall cosmic body was characteristically homogeneous. All that would later develop into sun, moon, earth, and planets was uniformly held in suspension and united into a single, nebular mass. Since the current planet Saturn still retains an atavistic remnant of this primeval condition, the first stage in the formation of the solar system is esoterically termed, the "Ancient Saturn Period," and the single, primeval sphere of warmth ether is known as "Old Saturn."[22]

While modern cosmologists certainly recognize cycles of expansion and collapse in the life of stars, this rhythmic principle does not appear to be an integral part of the nebular hypothesis of the solar system. To supersensible investigators, however, the formation of our solar system is characterized by cyclic activity; cyclic rhythms are fundamental to its development; and it could not have properly evolved without these alternating cycles.

The "cosmic activity" of the Ancient Saturn Period (in Sanskrit: "Manvantara") was, therefore, followed by a period of "cosmic rest" (in Sanskrit: "Pralaya"). During the human process of sleep, the astral and ego vehicles temporarily withdraw from the physical and etheric bodies in order to assimilate the day's experiences and to refresh body and soul. Similarly, the Ancient Saturn Period was brought to a cosmic completion by the withdrawal of all the advanced beings and elementary life-forms in and around Old Saturn into a united, supernal condition of soul and spirit. In consequence, all developmental activity connected with Old Saturn ceased, and the sphere of warmth ether slowly returned to its original, amorphous condition.

Furthermore, in conformity with the great cosmic cycles of expansion and contraction, the formation of our solar system also undergoes numerous rhythmic cycles of condensation and rarefaction. During the Ancient Saturn Period, for instance, the immense sphere of etheric warmth slowly congealed to more of a sense-perceptible heat. As the sphere gradually condensed, it also began to languidly rotate. Once again, these activities were not simply the result of blind, mechanical forces, but rather the deliberate effects of advanced beings in order to further the progress of life.

When the various beings and life-forms departed Old Saturn during the period of cosmic rest, the densified etheric sphere ceased rotating and contracting, thereby slowly reverting to its original, diffuse condition. Moreover, the vacated sphere of warmth ether did not dissipate into cosmic space, but analogous to the human body during sleep, it lay quietly dormant until the dawn of a new period of activity. Overall, this cyclic process of manifestation and dissolution, as occurred with Old Saturn, can also be likened to the solemn inbreathing and outbreathing of a gigantic, etheric organism.

7.4   The Second Stage: The "Ancient Sun Period"

When the vast company of beings and life-forms withdrew from outwardly participating in the etheric body of Old

Saturn and entered into an inward condition of soul and spirit, they did not disappear into nothingness. Nor was all the formational progress of these various beings and life-forms lost. Rather, all experience was retained as cosmic memory on the higher planes, and all beings and life-forms melted into a cosmic ocean of blissful oneness. During this period of restful latency, the various beings and life-forms continued to withdraw into their individual natures in order to assimilate their activity on Old Saturn and to transform this extract into future potential. In a cosmic sense, then, all the beings and life-forms associated with Old Saturn "seeded themselves."

In time, the period of cosmic rest came to an end as the "slumbering" beings of Old Saturn began to long for outward expression, for re-awakening. Once again, the various superphysical beings and life-forms gradually re-entered the waiting nebular sphere of etheric warmth, the dormant corpus of Old Saturn. Due to the evolutionary experience acquired on Old Saturn, the re-activated beings and life-forms quickly (relatively speaking, of course) transformed the warmth ether that had been left behind. In a sense, then, the early phase of this second period of planetary and solar development was an accelerated repetition or recapitulation of all that was achieved during the Ancient Saturn Period. Once this recapitulation had been established, then new evolutionary activity began to occur.

One of the most significant developments to occur during this second cosmic period was the condensation (cooling) of the entire pre-solar nebula of warmth ether into a more compact sphere of aeriform, vaporous material. This nebular condensation was accompanied by a corresponding rarefaction of the warmth ether into light ether (see Figure 11 below). In consequence, the large gaseous sphere began to glow—at first with an inner, supersensible light; then later with a faint, sense-perceptible light. Due to the nascent manifestation of light, this developmental stage is esoterically referred to as the "Ancient Sun Period" and the glowing, nebular sphere of gas is termed the "Old Sun." As with Old Saturn, the glowing, gaseous immensity of Old Sun contained all the embryonic ingredients of the present-day earth and the seven classical planets.

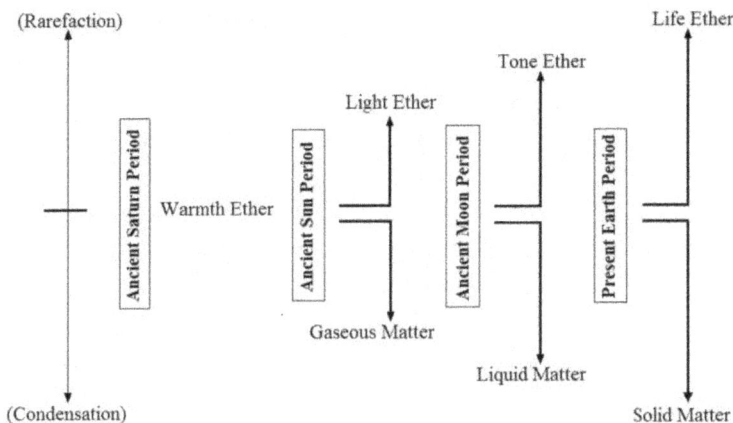

Figure 11: The Planetary Condensation of Matter and Rarefaction of the Ethers

Since the "spirits of wisdom (dominions)" had progressed up the evolutionary ladder through their participation in the life of Old Saturn, they could similarly perform what the higher spirits of will (thrones) did for the Ancient Saturn Period; that is, they could sacrifice a part of their etheric nature for the life development of other beings. In consequence, internally-generated life activity began to manifest within the gaseous sphere of Old Sun.

As permanent life-forms of warmth ether came into

existence on Old Saturn, permanent life-forms of gaseous material were slowly brought into being on Old Sun. As well, the rudimentary life-forms of warmth ether that were born on Old Saturn were re-awakened during the Ancient Sun Period and brought to a further state of development. During this second cosmic period, these life-forms were comprised of two substances instead of one: warmth ether *and* gaseous material. Moreover, into these dual substances was infused the light ether permanently bestowed by the spirits of wisdom. As a result, these life-forms now possessed an inner vitality; unlike the newly-generated, gaseous life-forms that were entirely directed by external forces (and beings). Furthermore, the lasting incorporation of light ether enabled these elementary life-forms to radiate a supersensible light. This in turn caused the gaseous sphere of Old Sun to supersensibly incandesce.

A further significant development to occur during the Ancient Sun Period was the separation of the unitary gaseous sphere into two. Some of the beings connected to Old Sun (particularly the undeveloped "principalities") had not entirely completed their necessary evolution on Old Saturn. Since these beings were unable to continue their retrograde Saturn activity in union with Old Sun, they caused a smaller sphere of warmth material to "spin off" from the main body. To sensory perception, this spin-off took the form of a flattened etheric ellipsoid, similar to a protoplanetary disk as envisioned by modern cosmologists. The occurrence, however, was not due to gravitation or centrifugal force but to the actions of supersensible beings.

Viewed externally, then, during this second ancient period of development in the life of our solar system, there existed a turning, pre-solar sphere of heated, glowing gas around which extended a secondary spheroid of retrograde material. Within the homogeneous substance of the large, central body was contained all that would later become the sun, earth, moon, and four additional planets. The secondary sphere would later become our current planet Saturn.

The supersensible details of Old Sun evolution are far more complex, expansive, profound and amazing than what has been briefly indicated here of course. Clairvoyant investigation has determined, for instance, that there are seven smaller cycles of "cosmic sleep" and "cosmic awakening" within each ancient period of development. Each of these smaller cycles has noteworthy events and activities that have contributed to the solar system that we see today; but which are far beyond the scope of this discourse (though well worth separate study).

7.5   The Third Stage: The "Ancient Moon Period"

As the beings and life-forms once again withdrew their outward activity from Old Sun and evanesced into a cosmic slumber, the separated planetary spheres correspondingly reunited into a single, homogeneous body once again.

> Everything that had developed on the [Old] Sun passed over into a state comparable to that of a plant when its growth forces lie dormant in the seed. Just as these forces of growth come to light again in a new plant, however, all of the [Old] Sun's life emerged from the womb of the cosmos again when the rest period was over, and a new planetary existence began. (Rudolf Steiner; *An Outline of Esoteric Science*)

When the various life-forms and beings re-emerged from their lengthy, embryonic interlude in the soul and spirit worlds, they once again entered into association with a nebular sphere of etheric warmth. Like the beginning of the Ancient Sun Period, the awaiting etheric warmth was rapidly transformed so that the foundational conditions of the

Ancient Saturn Period could be recapitulated. Moreover, as had occurred twice before, elementary life-forms composed of warmth ether were brought into being. These newly-differentiated life-forms, however, were slightly more developed than the ones established during the previous two periods due to the increased wisdom and ability that the formational beings had since acquired.

Subsequently, during what is supersensibly perceived to be a second phase of preparation for the third cosmic period, the nebular sphere of warmth ether condensed to a gaseous condition, thereby rarefacting a corresponding envelope of light ether. This phase, of course, was an accelerated recapitulation of the Ancient Sun Period. As also occurred on Old Sun, the warm, gaseous nebular sphere once again began to radiate an inner light. The gaseous life-forms that came into being on Old Sun were further developed and infused with an indwelling etheric vehicle which empowered these simple forms with inner vitality and life. Likewise, the life-forms that were established on Old Saturn were further perfected and re-infused with an improved etheric vehicle.

Unfortunately, at that time there were atavistic life-forms still existing at an Old Saturn stage of development who were unable to adapt to the new planetary conditions. Consequently, as occurred with Old Sun, an etheric portion was spun off from the main gaseous body to enable a more distanced, slower pace of development for these laggard life-forms. This detached sphere of ancient residue would much later metamorphose into today's planet Saturn.

Following a minor "cosmic rest," a third phase began that was not a recapitulation of previous planetary conditions. One of the new developments that occurred during this phase was the condensation of a large portion of the gaseous nebula into liquid matter. Once again, this resulted in the corresponding rarefaction of a more refined ether in and around the cosmic sphere; in this case, tone or sound ether.

The original nebular sphere was now a densified body of warm, moisture-laden gas that glowed and vibrated with supersensible sound. Spontaneously, the vibrational activity of sound (chemical) ether generated clearly-defined formations throughout the liquid material that would function as elementary life-forms. Of course this new planetary condition had a profound effect on all the beings and life-forms connected to it.

The process of condensation was brought about by the concurrent infusion of astral substance into the gaseous sphere. As the spirits of wisdom (dominions) had sacrificially bestowed a portion of their etheric nature for the further development of Old Sun, so the "spirits of movement (virtues)" had since acquired the capacity to sacrifice a portion of their astral nature to assist the life-forms developing during this third planetary period. This astral material was incorporated as a budding new vehicle for the life-forms that came into being on Old Saturn, and which now had a sufficiently-developed etheric vehicle to accommodate it.

Relatively soon after the condensation of liquid matter, another monumental planetary event occurred—the illuminated, central sphere split into two. Certain highly-advanced beings, such as the "spirits of form (powers)," were unable to properly develop in connection with the existing sphere. In order to accelerate their evolution, they spun off the denser gaseous and liquid material as a separately-revolving, planetary sphere; thereby establishing for themselves a suitable cosmic body of lighter gaseous material that was suffused with heat and light.

As a result, the spun-off, gas-permeated spheroid of liquid no longer radiated light outwardly into space; it could only reflect the light streaming to it from the detached, brightly-illuminated, gaseous sphere—like a liquid, lunar mirror. It was partly due to this reflective characteristic that esoteric science has termed this watery sphere, "Old Moon," and the entire third stage of primeval development for our solar system is referred to as the "Ancient Moon Period." Moreover, similar to the ancient residue "inherited" by today's planet Saturn, some vestigial remnant of Old Moon forces and beings has also been preserved with today's moon.

The Ancient Moon Period of solar system development, then, was characterized by three distinct planetary bodies: a gigantic, incandescent, pre-solar sphere around which revolved a large, reflective, gas-permeated, liquid spheroid; and a small, dense, gaseous spheroid of residue from Old Saturn. Each of these celestial bodies provided the appropriate evolutionary arena the various life-forms and advanced beings associated with our world.

The liquid, Old Moon sphere contained the combined material of what would separately become the earth and the moon during the next (fourth) great period of solar and planetary development. Not surprisingly, once the higher vibrational forces and substances withdrew to form a pre-solar cosmic body, the overall material of Old Moon rapidly densified. It is important to keep in mind at this point in esoteric cosmogony, that the mineral kingdom as we know it did not yet exist. Therefore, the lowest material densification of Old Moon was not to the degree of hardness exhibited by our present-day minerals. Rather, certain areas on the liquid surface of Old Moon densified to the level of thick cartilage or soft wood.

While much more esoteric information is available concerning the life and development of Old Moon, this is not considered necessary for the purposes of this brief summary. Suffice to say that, once again, this ancient period of planetary evolution cyclically passed into cosmic repose.

7.6   The Fourth Stage: The "Present Earth Period"

Viewed supersensibly, the more powerful beings associated with the central, pre-solar sphere powerfully gathered all the distanced life-forms and beings back into a vast exaltation of unity in the higher planes of soul and spirit. As a result, all the detached substances and forces on the material and etheric planes once again recombined into a single, homogeneous, nebular mass in preparation for a new, fourth period of planetary evolution.

To esoteric science, it is only this fourth period of solar system development that is empirically investigated by modern cosmogony and formulated with the nebular hypothesis. Since the three previous planetary periods are only open to supersensible investigation, they are obviously not recognized by physical science. It is during this fourth period that our present-day earth planet has come into being and, therefore, this stage is esoterically referred to as the "Present Earth Period" or simply the "Earth Period."

CHAPTER 8

THE PRESENT PERIOD OF THE EARTH AND SOLAR SYSTEM

8.1   The First Recapitulation Phase: The "Polarian Age"

AS ENVISIONED BY the nebular hypothesis, our present solar system began as a vast, diffuse nebula; but according to esoteric science, not as a nebula of interstellar dust, but as a nebula of etheric warmth—another recapitulation of the Ancient Saturn Period. During the first recapitulation phase of the Earth Period (termed the "Polarian Age" by esoteric science), before any atavistic residue of material and forces were spun off to form Saturn, even more primeval substance was flung outwardly to accommodate extremely primitive life-forms that had become associated with our original nebular mass.[23] This detachment would condense in time to form our present-day planet of Uranus.

Shortly thereafter, the throwback etheric forces and material that would later densify to form our present-day planet of Saturn were also spun off for use by other recalcitrant life-forms. At that time, the remaining central nebular sphere still contained all that would later become sun, earth, moon, and the other planets. Near the end of this first recapitulation, a faint glow was emitted from the enormous central sphere; otherwise, all was in darkness.

8.2 The Second Recapitulation Phase: The "Hyperborean Age"

During the second phase of the Earth Period, which is esoterically termed the "Hyperborean Age," the Ancient Sun Period was recapitulated. This was at a much higher level, of course, since evolutionary progress is not simply going around in endless, self-same circles; but instead, it is circling ever upward in spiralling advancement.

Once again, there came a time when many exalted beings could no longer continue their accelerated development in close connection with the lesser life-forms existing within the central nebular sphere. By separating off the more refined gaseous, heat and light material from the general mass, they were able to re-establish a suitable pre-solar sphere of activity for their advanced evolution. This material distancing was also necessary for the lesser life-forms that were spun off with the denser material since they correspondingly required a slower pace for their proper development.

After this time, life-sustaining light from this nascent sun shone out externally upon the lesser life-forms associated with the three detached planetary spheres. Shortly thereafter, from the sphere that was closest to the infant sun, residue from the Ancient Sun Period was also spun off in order to establish what would later become the planet Jupiter. As described by Rudolf Steiner in *An Outline of Esoteric Science*:

> There were souls who found no place on [the sphere that contained our] Earth already at the time when the [infant] Sun separated from the [composite] Earth. They were removed to another planet to develop further. Under the

guidance of cosmic beings, this planet detached itself from the general mass of the cosmos that was still united with the Earth at the beginning of its physical evolution. (The Sun had already disconnected itself.) This planet is the one whose physical expression is known to outer science as Jupiter.

From the quotation above, we should also note that while the various planetary spheres that were spun off from the central sun were evolutionary arenas for lesser-developed beings and life-forms, they were also accompanied by highly-advanced beings who were responsible for overall planetary formation, rotation, revolution and alignment. These are the beings respectively known as the "spirits of form, the spirits of movement, the spirits of wisdom and the cherubim." The seraphim have the responsibility of supersensibly connecting our entire solar system with other planetary systems in the galaxy.

At this point in the Hyperborean Age, the solar system consisted of five celestial spheres: (1) an embryonic, fiery sun comprised of rarefied gaseous material that radiated heat and light; (2) a denser, hot, gaseous sphere that would later condense to become planet earth; which was still united to the material and forces that would later become our moon; (3) the planet Jupiter; (4) the planet Saturn; and (5) the planet Uranus.

8.3 The Third Recapitulation Phase: The "Lemurian Age"

Once the rarified gaseous and etheric material had been separated off to form the vestigial sun, much of the heated, aeriform substance of the composite earth and moon sphere rapidly condensed to a steamy, vaporous condition—a recapitulation of what had taken place during the Ancient

Moon Period. A corresponding rarefaction of sound (chemical) ether also occurred at this time, permeating the steamy earth-moon sphere with currents of supersensible sound.

As the earth-moon sphere was condensing from its previous gaseous condition, a sixth planetary body was separated off from the sun. Rather than remain rotationally closer to the central body, as would be logically expected, this mass of rarified material actually passed through the earth-moon sphere to a distance between it and Jupiter. This mysterious sphere would later densify to become the planet Mars. As described by Rudolf Steiner in a lecture in 1908 (published in *The Influence of Spiritual Beings Upon Man*; 1961):

> The sun pressed out and we have now sun, with earth and moon together. During this time Mars—in a way which would take too much time to relate now in detail—had again formed a theatre for particular beings, and in its further advance Mars actually passed through the earth and moon and left behind what today we know as iron.

It is important to remember in connection with the separation of Mars from the sun, that all planetary separations begin as flattened, circular, etheric extensions that stretch out from the sun to the orbital distance of today's planetary globe. These protoplanetary etheric disks have been established in our solar system primarily through the actions of the progressive spirits of form (powers). The planetary globes that we perceive in space today are densified concretions that were later formed at the outer margins of the original etheric disks primarily through the actions of regressive spirits of form (see Figure 12 below).

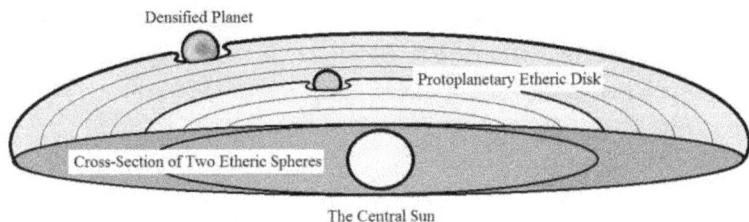

Figure 12: Planetary Formation According to Esoteric Science

The passage of Mars through the earth-moon planetary sphere was therefore not in the manner of a densified planetary collision, but rather in the manner of a spinning, outward expansion of rarified, etheric force and material. This higher-vibrational Martian material easily interpenetrated the denser earth-moon sphere, and just as easily stretched far beyond it.

The further accelerated evolution connected with the sun that resulted from the extrusion of Mars soon proved too rapid and intense for two other advanced life-forms. Certain archangelic beings were the first to depart by spinning off the planetary sphere known today as Venus (the ancient Mercury). Sometime later, certain principalities (time-spirits) likewise had to distance their development from the sun by spinning off the planetary sphere known today as Mercury (the ancient Venus). As elaborated, once again, by Rudolf Steiner:

> [There] were certain beings which had not ascended high enough to be able to endure the sun existence ... Dwelling places had to be created for them. None of the other [planetary] theatres could have served them, for those were for beings of another nature ... [who] had not quite kept up with them in cosmic evolution ... Mercury

and Venus are two planets which have split off as the centres for those Fire-Spirits [Archangels and Principalities] who are exalted far above human existence, yet who could not have supported the sun-existence. (Ibid)

8.4   The Separation of the Moon

At first, the separation of the high-vibrational sun forces beneficially decreased the rapid pace of advancement for the less-developed life-forms connected to the earth-moon sphere; but over time the planetary union of earth and moon became seriously detrimental to the various evolving life-forms existing there. Atavistic, etheric moon forces were soon causing serious atrophication in the bodily vehicles of the progressive life-forms associated with the earth. As a result, around the middle of the Lemurian Age, the degenerative moon forces were spun outwardly from the main body of the liquid and aeriform earth to the orbital distance of today's lunar globe.

The extrusion of the lunar sphere, therefore, should not be understood as the physical ejection of a solid orb from a hardened, mineralized earth body. In fact, according to esoteric science, the mineral kingdom on earth only came into existence *after* the extrusion of the moon. With the outward distancing of the stultifying moon forces from the sphere of the earth, a further condensation and rarefaction process immediately occurred: liquid substance densified to a solid condition, and sound ether rarified to life ether (refer back to Figure 11).

Over time, with the increasing solidification and mineralization of the earth, the planetary sphere became a fiery, molten mass in space. Moreover, the rarified, interpenetrating, life ether caused the magmatic material to exhibit a life-like, seething activity. As the surface of the molten earth slowly cooled, temporary islands of hardened material would appear and disappear in the fiery broiling. Not surprisingly, the first, large permanent land-mass to cool was continually wracked by volcanic activity. This was the fiery continent referred to in esoteric science as "Lemuria."

8.5 The Sun, Moon and Planets as Macrocosmic Vehicles of Expression

By the end of the Lemurian Age, then, our solar system had evolved the basic configuration that we are familiar with today. Of course there continued to be planetary adjustments and realignments, as well as additional densifications to the orbiting globes, even into the following age. While esoteric details are sparse concerning the solar acquisitions of Neptune and Pluto, presumably these also occurred during the Lemurian Age.

While modern astronomy has certainly presented us with wondrously-beautiful, awe-inspiring photographs of the cosmos—the planets, the stars, the constellations and the galaxies—sadly undermining this emotional exaltation is the scientific worldview that the entire universe is lifeless, purposeless, insensate and amoral. All this cosmic beauty is just mechanical, chemical activity that has no meaning.

To esoteric science, however, the supersensible universe is teeming with life, consciousness and being; in fact, the universe itself *is* a breathtakingly-majestic, cosmic being—the Logos-Word. All the spectacular planetary, lunar, solar, stellar, galactic and supergalactic phenomena that are empirically observed throughout the vast universe are actually the physical expressions of countless intelligent, powerful and purposeful beings.

The various moons and planets of our own solar system

are not simply lifeless, chemical orbs inanimately moving through sterile space, but rather the vehicles of expression for highly-advanced beings. In the same way that human beings incorporate a number of microcosmic, interpenetrating vehicles of expression, the various lunar, planetary and solar beings manifest themselves through macrocosmic globes of expression.

This supersensible fact was certainly known in ancient times due to the dream-like clairvoyance that humanity still retained. In Roman mythology, for example, Mars, Mercury, Venus, Saturn, Jupiter, Apollo (the sun), and Diana (the moon) were all gods who shone down from the dome of heaven; they were not simply lifeless orbs in space. Likewise in ancient Greece, in ancient India and in ancient Babylonia (see Figure 12 below). Though these ancients mythologies often had more than one name for these planetary deities, nevertheless, the intention was clear: these planetary orbs were ensouled by higher, more advanced beings. Interestingly, these ancient planetary deities were characteristically either masculine or feminine. The ensouling deity of planet earth, for example, was usually regarded as a feminine being: she was Ceres to the Romans, Demeter to the Greeks, Shakti to the Hindus, and Damkina to the Babylonians.

Somewhat similar to microcosmic life-forms, the celestial orbs not only have a spherical, planetary-size physical vehicle, but also interpenetrating, planetary-size etheric and astral vehicles. Planetary orbs, however, do not have an indwelling ego or infused higher vehicles. The ego-being of a planet (which in this case includes the moon) is a power, an elohim-being. Normally, the elohim-beings who act as "planetary-egos" or "planetary-spirits" operate from the supersensible sphere of the sun. The planetary spirit of the moon is an exception, however, since this elohim-being operates from the periphery of the lunar orb itself.[24]

Perhaps not surprisingly, the presiding ego-being of the

sun is at a level more highly advanced than a planetary power. The "spirit of the sun" is not an elohim-being but rather a "virtue or dynameis." In our own solar system, then, there are seven major elohim (spirits of form) and one powerful virtue (spirit of movement) providing the external egoic vehicles for sun, moon and planets.

PLANETS	ROMAN GODS	GREEK GODS	HINDU GODS	BABYLONIAN GODS
SUN	Apollo	Helios	Surya	Shamash
MOON	Diana	Artemis	Chandra	Sin
MERCURY	Mercury	Hermes	Budha	Nabu
VENUS	Venus	Aphrodite	Shukra	Ishtar
MARS	Mars	Ares	Mangala	Nergal
JUPITER	Jupiter	Zeus	Brihaspati	Marduk
SATURN	Saturn	Chronus	Shani	Ninib
EARTH	Ceres	Demeter	Shakti	Damkina

Figure 12: The Planetary Deities in Ancient Mythology

8.6 The Seven Classical Planets According to Esoteric Science

It should be obvious, at this point, that most of the ancient mythologies only included seven celestial spheres (other than the earth, of course) as members of our solar system. These have come to be known as "the seven classical planets" of antiquity. The prosaic explanation for this is that these "wandering" celestial orbs (in Greek: "planētēs") were the only ones readily visible to the unaided eye. It is commonly contended that Uranus, Neptune and Pluto are only visible with a telescope and, therefore, were not known to ancient observers.[25]

Sounds reasonable enough, even though it is actually possible to see Uranus and Neptune in a clear, dark sky without a telescope if one knows where to look. Moreover, Hindu mythology includes two additional "shadow" planets, Raahu and Ketu. As well, the Sumerians numbered twelve "celestial bodies" to our solar system: the sun, the moon, and ten planets. As for Pluto, even modern astronomy no longer recognizes it as a true planet, but now designates it as a "dwarf."

According to esoteric tradition, the reason ancient mythologies did not acknowledge additional planets beyond Saturn was that Uranus, Neptune and Pluto were considered to be temporary "acquisitions"; that is, planets that were added *after* the original formation of our solar system, which extended only to the orbital boundary of Saturn. As explained by Theosophical writer, Andrew Rooke:

> In theosophy Uranus, Neptune, and Pluto differ from the sacred planets which latter are closely related with the destiny of earth. They do not strictly belong to our solar system, but have been captured by the gravitational energy of the sun. Although Uranus belongs to our "universal solar system," and is intimately linked with the destiny of the sun, Neptune, and perhaps Pluto, ventured into the outer reaches of our system, possibly during the chaos of solar and planetary formation billions of years ago (cf. *Fountain-Source,* pp. 324-5). Theosophists compare this process with the micro-universe of the atom that captures and discards electrons. Similarly, Neptune, and perhaps Pluto, will one day leave the solar system. However, as in the atomic world, Pluto, and especially Neptune, vitally affect the "magnetism" of the solar system and thus life here on earth billions of miles away. (From "Sunrise" magazine; 1987)

Anthroposophist Rudolf Steiner, not surprisingly,

maintained this esoteric position as well:

> It is to be noted that the two outermost planets now reckoned as belonging to our system by physical astronomy—Uranus and Neptune—did not originally belong to our Solar System; they came much later into the sphere of attraction of our system: they then joined company and remained with it. They cannot therefore be reckoned in the same sense as the other planets as belonging to our system from Saturn onwards, for they, so to speak, belonged to it from the beginning. (Lecture in 1912 from *The Spiritual Beings in the Heavenly Bodies and the Kingdoms of Nature*; 2011)

8.7   The Continent of Lemuria

The Lemurian Age, then, does not just refer to the prehistoric continent of Lemuria, as is often mistakenly conveyed in Theosophical literature. Moreover, the fiery beginnings of the Lemurian continent were entirely inhospitable to physical life as we know it. It was only near the very end of the Lemurian Age that sense-perceptible life-forms existed *on* the surface of the continent. Prior to that time, life-forms could only exist in a rarified, etheric condition invisibly suspended *above* the volcanic surface of the floating land-mass.

Once the mineral kingdom had begun to crystallize on earth, elementary plant forms came into existence, and then rudimentary animal forms after that. As well, primitive human forms (that would be considered grotesque today) chemically materialized for the very first time on the ancient Lemurian continent.

8.8   The Birth of Humanity on Earth

The first-time appearance of mineralized human forms on ancient Lemuria does not mean that human life-forms did not exist prior to that time. According to esoteric science, though human life-forms were the last to sense-perceptibly appear on Lemuria, they were actually life-forms that were far older than minerals, plants or animals. In fact, elementary human life-forms first came into existence during the Ancient Saturn Period of planetary formation. These were the life-forms that further acquired an etheric vehicle during the Ancient Sun Period, and an astral vehicle during the Ancient Moon Period.

During our Present Earth Period, it took the three recapitulation phases of the Polarian Age, the Hyperborean Age and most of the Lemurian Age to further develop and prepare the physical, etheric and astral vehicles of the human life-forms in order for them to receive the great gift of a permanent soul vehicle.[26] With the bestowal of enduring soul-substance as a sacrificial gift from the progressive powers (the elohim or spirits of form), human life-forms acquired the beginnings of self-conscious awareness. The first, faint stirrings of self-awareness enkindled the spark of the ego, the individual "I." With ego-awareness came personhood. Our animal-like, ancestral human *life-forms* on Lemuria had now become human *beings.*

As human beings, then, our physical bodies began as a sacrificial gift of warmth ether from the thrones (spirits of will) during the Ancient Saturn Period.[27] Our etheric (or life) body began as a sacrificial gift from the dominions (spirits of wisdom) during the Ancient Sun Period. Our astral (or emotional) body began as a sacrificial gift from the virtues (spirits of movement) during the Ancient Moon Period.

During the Present Earth Period, we owe the gift of individual egohood (self) to the sacrificial outpouring of the powers, the elohim (spirits of form). To esoteric science, then, human beings are not simply the random formations of blind, chemical forces; but rather, the complex living offspring of numerous celestial beings existing within the Logos-Word. Most of these advanced beings have faithfully acted in accordance with the divine impulses of the Trinitarian God; some, however, have acted in opposition. Humanity, as we exist on earth today, is the astonishing result.

At the close of the Lemurian Age, the various sense-perceptible life-forms that we are familiar with on earth: mineral, plant, animal and human—had also become firmly established (though their outer appearance was exceedingly primitive when compared with the beautifully complex forms of today). Even though humanity had acquired the first, seminal stirrings of self-conscious awareness during the Lemurian Age, it was really only during the following "Atlantean Age" that individual ego-awareness began to significantly unfold in the human soul.

CONCLUSION

CONCLUDING *The Greater Mysteries of the Divine Trinity, the Logos-Word and Creation* with the birth of humanity on earth may appear somewhat abrupt and perhaps incomplete. Nevertheless, the esoteric history of humanity on earth rightly deserves a detailed discourse of its own. Echoing traditional Church theology, the esoteric Christian history of mankind is the "story of salvation": the fall from supernatural grace; the expulsion from heavenly paradise; the descent into materiality and spiritual darkness; the raising up of a chosen people as preparation for a messiah; the incarnation of Christ-Jesus; the overcoming of sin, sickness, evil and death; and the establishment of a "new heaven and a new earth."

Indeed, the sources of esoteric Christianity have a great deal to share today concerning the greater mysteries of salvation history, which in essence are the greater mysteries of the person of Christ-Jesus. For those who are interested, much of this mystery-information is included in an extensive follow-up discourse entitled, *The Star of Higher Knowledge: The Five Guiding Mysteries of Esoteric Christianity.*

NOTES

INTRODUCTION

1. Though there are a variety of meanings for the term, "theosophy," what is here meant is the systematic study of the divine using various supersensible means of investigation (such as "reading the akashic record").

CHAPTER 2

2. The unique functions of the universal masculine and universal feminine principles are plainly manifested in a biological way by human reproduction. The comparatively large and expansive female ovum remains in a state of receptive latency until fertilized by the comparatively small but mobile male seed. Once internally excited by the singular, male seed impulse, the enlivened feminine forces of propagation rapidly undertake, from start to completion, the astoundingly complex process of human generation.

CHAPTER 3

3. Certain Gnostic writings such as the Sethian text, *Trimorphic Protennoia*, profess a trinity of Father, Son and feminine spirit Sophia; also denoted as God the Father, Sophia the Mother and Logos the Son. The association of Gnosticism with the idea of a feminine Holy Spirit may well have contributed to the rejection of "God the Mother" by later Christian theologians. Interestingly, St. Augustine rejected a Trinity of Father, Son and Mother partly on the basis that "such things may be offensive in carnal affairs by arousing thoughts of physical conceptions and births."

4. The association of divine motherhood and cosmic immanence has also been recognized by the Catholic Church, as expressed in the aforementioned quotation from the *Catechism*:

    > God's parental tenderness can also be expressed by the image of motherhood, which emphasizes God's immanence, the intimacy between Creator and creation.

5. As Christ addressed the "Lord's Prayer" to the transcendent Heavenly Father, a similar prayer, such as the following, could be addressed to the immanent Holy Mother:

    PRAYER TO OUR HOLY MOTHER

    Our Mother, who shines in matter;
    Hallowed be thy forms.
    Thy wisdom lives;
    Thy wisdom shapes the earth as well as the heavens.
    Form for us the day and our daily bread;
    And forgive us our defilement,
    As we forgive those who defile against you.

And keep us from material temptation,
And the error of thinking that matter is evil.
For the beauty, the grace and the honour are yours,
Now and forever,

AMA*/AMEN

* (AMA is the Kabbalistic name for the divine Mother:
see S. L. MacGregor Mathers; *The Kabbalah Unveiled*; 1983)

6. As one of the "Certain Truths Not Yet Defined by the Magisterium," the Catholic Church maintains that "The Holy Ghost proceeds from the will or from the mutual love of the Father and of the Son." As further elaborated by John Paul II in a General Audience (November 20, 1985):

> The Father who begets loves the Son who is begotten. The Son loves the Father with a love which is identical with that of the Father. In the unity of the divinity, love is on one side paternal and on the other, filial. At the same time the Father and the Son are not only united by that mutual love as two Persons infinitely perfect. But their mutual gratification, their reciprocal love, proceeds in them and from them as a person. The Father and the Son "spirate" the Spirit of Love consubstantially with them. In this way God, in the absolute unity of the divinity, is from all eternity Father, Son and Holy Spirit.

7. The symbol of the triangle with the "all-seeing eye" is a respectful reminder that these diagrams are not merely abstractions, but represent the three divine persons of God. Though this symbol has been co-opted by Freemasonry since the late eighteenth century, it was originally a Christian symbol commonly used in Medieval and Renaissance Europe.

8. "Goodness," or moral virtue, can be regarded as rightful

action or the wisdom-filled application of the will. As St. Thomas Aquinas has expressed:

> Since good as perceived by intellect is the object of the will, it is impossible for God to will anything but what his wisdom approves. (*Summa Theologica*)

Likewise, as indicated diagrammatically, "mercy" can be regarded as the loving application of the will; and "compassion" or empathy can be regarded as wisdom suffused with love.

9. Another equally correct way of understanding how the divine capacity to create arises out of the personal relationship of the Trinity is to say that the Heavenly Father and the Holy Mother do not create *directly*; but by eternally begetting the Son, they *indirectly* share in the Son's capacity to create *through* their consummate union with the Son.

CHAPTER 4

10. Esoterically understood, the "burning bush" of Moses is the fiery red, multi-branching blood system of the human body. Through initiation, the higher spirit-self—the "I AM"—is able to declare itself from out of the radiating blood-heat that enlivens the body, but "does not consume."

11. The divine process of mutual self-knowing through the gendered unification of the Heavenly Father and the Holy Mother is correspondingly reflected in limited human experience. This is conveyed in the language of Old Testament scripture in such passages as, "Now Adam *knew* Eve his wife, and she conceived and bore Cain ..." (Gen 4:1). While "knowing" in this instance is clearly associated with sexual union, divine self-knowing, of

course, infinitely transcends human sexuality.

12. Interestingly, while Catholic theology also maintains that the Word is the mental image of God, this created image is also incongruously equated with God the Son. The illustrious doctor of the Church, St. Thomas Aquinas, perfected and popularized the "psychological analogy of the Trinity," first introduced by St. Augustine in *De Trinitate* (399–422). Aquinas' explanation of the Trinity in *Summa Theologica* (which has been widely accepted by Catholic theologians), is based on the idea that the internal relationship of Father, Son and Holy Spirit is analogous to the subjective activity of thought and will in the human mind. The begetting of the Son from the Father was, according to Aquinas, analogous to the generation of a concept in the human mind. In this sense, the Son was understood to be a divine "Verbum Mentale," a divine "Word Concept."

To Aquinas, then, the Son was identical to the Word. The logical problem with equating the Son with a divine idea, however, is that ideas, whether human or divine, are mental formulations that have a temporal beginning as well as a finite delineation and meaning. This, of course, cannot apply in any respect to the personal nature of God. Analogously, it would be just as incongruous to maintain that a mirrored reflection is completely identical to a real person. As previously explained, the eternal generation of the Son is more correctly in the manner of arousing self-conscious awareness within the mind of God; whereas the creation of the Logos-Word is more in the manner of cognitively formulating a mental concept within the mind of God—two enormously different processes.

13. Surprisingly echoing Heraclitus' conception of an impersonal Logos, on 1 April 2005, Cardinal Joseph Ratzinger (who would later become Pope Benedict XVI)

wrote:

> From the beginning, Christianity has understood itself
> as the religion of the Logos, as the religion according
> to reason ... we Christians must be very careful to
> remain faithful to this fundamental line; to live a faith
> that comes from the Logos, from creative reason.

CHAPTER 5

14. We are dealing here, of course, with aeons of cosmic
time; but the point being made is that compared to the
vast stretches of time involved in the vibratory re-ascent
of the Word, the initial vibratory descent was
comparatively rapid.

CHAPTER 6

15. The Western theological ordering of superphysical beings
into three main categories each containing three
subdivisions (nine levels in total) was first made public in
a fifth-century writing entitled, *De Coelesti
Hierarchia* (*Celestial Hierarchy*) by Pseudo-Dionysius. This
ordering was later popularized by St. Thomas Aquinas in
Summa Theologica (1265–1274). Anthroposophy regards
Pseudo-Dionysius as a later student of Dionysius the
Areopagite, the founder of the Pauline school of esoteric
Christianity in Athens in the first century.
16. Most of the designations used in the Hebrew Tradition
section of the chart in Figure 9 are from the *Mishneh Torah*
(1170–1180) written by Moses Maimonides. A tenth level
of beings, the "erelim" were not included in the chart
since they are sometimes considered synonymous with
the ishim. Furthermore, although the ten designations of

Maimonides were ranked according to the nearness to God (like the other three sections of the chart), they were not originally arranged into three main hierarchies.

17. Humanity can be classified as the highest level of a fourth hierarchy, and the current mineral kingdom can be classified as the highest level of a fifth hierarchy, as illustrated in the following chart:

FOURTH HIERARCHY	HUMANS
	ANIMALS
	PLANTS
FIFTH HIERARCHY	MINERALS
	ATOMIC PARTICLES
	SUB-ATOMIC PARTICLES

18. The fact that the cosmic outpouring of the Logos-Word is differentiated into three great realms or worlds is not arbitrary or accidental, but rather another instance of the universal principle of "triplism": "All manifestations throughout the universe—from the highest to the lowest—reflect the Trinitarian nature of God the Creator."

19. Einstein, during his own life, did not entirely avoid using the term, "ether," in favour of the term, "space." As recorded by physicist and mathematician, Max Born (1882–1970):

> Einstein in later years proposed calling empty space equipped with gravitational and electromagnetic fields the "ether," whereby, however, this word is not to denote a substance with traditional attributes ... Such a use of the word "ether" is of course admissible, and

when once it has been sanctioned by usage in this way, probably quite convenient. From now on ether as a substance [with mechanical properties] vanishes from theory. (*Einstein's Theory of Relativity*. 1962)

20. Steiner's supersensible investigations contend that the sun has an empty, etheric centre:

> The sun is not a ball of gas; but in that place where the sun is, there is something less than empty space—a sucking, absorbing body, in fact, while all around it is that which exerts pressure. Consequently what comes to us from the sun is nothing to do with any product of combustion in the sun, but is a reflection, a raying back of all that the universe has rayed into it ... Where the sun is, is emptier than empty space. This can be said of all parts of the universe where we find ether. (*Mystery of the Universe: The Human Being, Image of Creation*; 2001)

Interestingly, the American Astronomical Society currently maintains that every large galaxy, including the Milky Way, has a supermassive black hole at its centre. As well, it is now theorized that black holes (that is, regions of empty space) can range in size from the cosmically colossal to the sub-atomically minuscule.

CHAPTER 7

21. As stated by Rudolf Steiner:

> The modified Kant-Laplace theory [the "nebular hypothesis"] may definitely hold good as an external event, but within the whole forming of globes, within this whole crystallizing of the separate cosmic globes, spiritual forces and spiritual beings were at work."

(The Influence of Spiritual Beings Upon Man; 1961)

22. Since the germinal constituents of present-day earth were homogeneously united with the entire sphere of Old Saturn, anthroposophical spiritual science also refers to Old Saturn as a previous "incarnation" of the earth:

> Before the Earth became the planet we know, it was a very different one. At the beginning of time it was a planet called, in occult science, [Old] Saturn. Altogether there have been four successive incarnations of the Earth: [Old] Saturn, [Old] Sun, [Old] Moon and Earth. (Rudolf Steiner; Lecture Nine: "Evolution of the Earth," 1906; published in *At the Gates of Spiritual Science*)

CHAPTER 8

23. Information given by Rudolf Steiner indicates that backward Uranian life-forms became associated with our solar system at the very end of the Ancient Moon Period, prior to the interval of cosmic sleep:

> For the beings who arose last of all during the [Ancient] Moon existence, and who therefore had stayed behind at a very early evolutionary stage, a field of action had to be separated out. This scene of action was the cosmic body which we call "Uranus," and which therefore has but slight connection with our earthly existence. Uranus has become the theatre for beings which had to remain at a very backward stage.

24. Anthroposophical research has also indicated that there are abnormal powers (retrograde virtues) who are also involved with planetary evolution. These abnormal

planetary spirits operate within the peripheries of Venus, Mercury, Mars, Jupiter and Saturn. In the words of Rudolf Steiner:

> [W]e must imagine that a certain sun-force, which streams towards us in the normal Spirits of Form, is altered by the force that streams to us from the abnormal Spirits of Form, who are really Spirits of Motion. These have their centre in the other five planets, speaking of the planets in the old way. You must therefore seek for the centre of these others, the abnormal Spirits of Form, in Saturn, Jupiter, Mars, Venus, Mercury. ("Lecture Six": *The Mission of the Individual Folk Souls in relation to Teutonic Mythology*; 2005)

Moreover, on earth there is a "fallen" power, a being abnormally acting as a principality within the supersensible sphere of the earth, who falsely claims to be the "spirit of this world." This retrograde elohim-being is the one widely known as Satan, Mephistopheles or Ahriman. As explained in "Lecture Seven" (1908) in *The Influence of Spiritual Beings Upon Man* (1961):

> Concealed behind the Original Forces [Principalities], therefore, are some who could actually be Powers, and among the Original Forces who have really no right to be there is that being whom one is right in calling "Satan"—Satan, the "Unlawful Prince of this World" ... He expresses himself by continually bringing confusion into man's relation to the Time-Spirit [one of the principalities], by bringing men to contradict the Epochal Spirit. That is the true nature of the Spirit who is also called the "Spirit of Darkness," or the Unlawful Prince of our Earth, he who claims to be the actual guide and leader of men.

25. Though the actual outer planets of Uranus, Neptune and
    Pluto may have been unknown to certain ancient cultures,
    some nevertheless recognized "celestial spheres" that
    were beyond the boundary of our own solar system but
    were connected to it in some way. As explained by Rudolf
    Steiner:

> Then we consider yet another planet, one not known
> to the ancient Hebrews. They were, however, aware
> of its sphere, which they thought of as beyond the
> planets; they thought of it as the crystal sphere that
> formed the vault of the heavens. Much later it was
> discovered that one could speak of Uranus as being
> there. But we can consider Uranus, even though it
> was discovered much later. The only difference is that
> the ancient Hebrews thought of a sphere in the place
> where Uranus was later located. (Lecture from 1916
> in *The Riddle of Humanity*)

26. In the words of Rudolf Steiner given in a 1910 lecture
    entitled "The Entrance of the Christ-being into the
    Evolution of Humanity":

> We know that the implanting of the ego in man is
> part of the collective development of the earth. The
> earth passed through the [Ancient] Saturn, Sun and
> Moon ages and then only did it become the structure
> it is today. On [Ancient] Saturn the germ of the
> physical body was laid, on the [Ancient] Sun that of
> the etheric body, on the [Ancient] Moon that of the
> astral body, and the germ of the ego was added on the
> earth; this germ was placed in the development of the
> earth in the Lemurian epoch. (Contained in the book:
> *The Christ Impulse and Development of the Ego-
> Consciousness*; 2010)

27. Though the substance of humanity's embryonic physical

body was gifted by the thrones during the Ancient Saturn Period, it was actually the powers who shaped and molded the warmth ether substance into a definite form (hence their esoteric name: the "spirits of form"). As described by Rudolf Steiner in a lecture in 1908:

> So it was with the Spirits of Form in the environment of ancient Saturn. They sent their life-bestowing saps down into the warmth masses of Saturn and their own form, their likenesses, was reflected; this mirror likeness was the first rudiments of the human physical body (published in *The Influence of Spiritual Beings Upon Man*; 1961).

Furthermore, it was these same powers (elohim) who later gave definite form to the embryonic etheric and astral substances that were sacrificed to the primeval human life-forms during the Ancient Sun and Ancient Moon Periods.

SELECT BIBLIOGRAPHY

(in alphabetical order)

- *Catechism of the Catholic Church*, (Random House, 2003)

- George Gamow, *One Two Three ... Infinity* (Dover Publications, 1988)

- H.P. Blavatsky, *The Secret Doctrine* (Cambridge University Press, 2011)

- Magus Incognito, *The Secret Doctrine of the Rosicrucians* (Yoga Publication Society, 1949)

- Rudolf Steiner, *An Outline of Occult Science* (Anthroposophic Press, 1989)

- Rudolf Steiner, *The Christian Mystery* (SteinerBooks, 1998)

- Rudolf Steiner, *The Course of My Life* (Anthroposophic Press, 1970)

- Rudolf Steiner, *The Influence of Spiritual Beings Upon Man* (Anthroposophic Press, 1961)

- Rudolf Steiner, *Theosophy* (SteinerBooks, 1994)

- Rudolf Steiner, *The Spiritual Beings in the Heavenly Bodies and the Kingdoms of Nature* (SteinerBooks, 2011)

- Saint Thomas Aquinas, *Summa Theologica* (Hayes Barton Press, 1999)

- The Holy Bible, *RSV-CE* (Ignatius Press, 1994)

- Three Initiates, *The Kybalion: A Study of Hermetic Philosophy of Ancient Egypt and Greece* (Kessinger Publishing, 2010)

- Yogi Ramacharaka, *Raja Yoga or Mental Development* (Indo-European Publishing, 2007)

- Yogi Ramacharaka, *The Yoga of Wisdom: Lessons in Gnani Yoga* (Interactive Media, 2013)

OTHER BOOKS BY

RON MACFARLANE

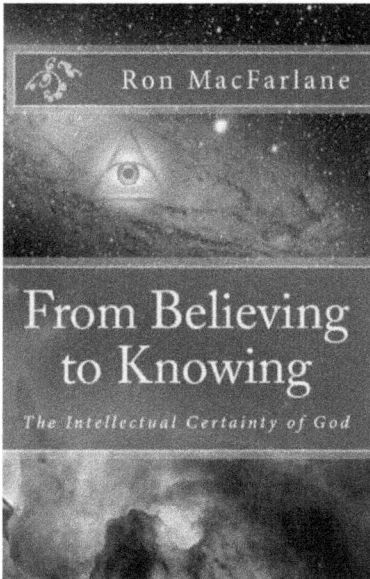

Ron MacFarlane

From Believing to Knowing

The Intellectual Certainty of God

THERE IS a puzzling and pervasive misconception in present-day thinking that the existence of God cannot be intellectually determined, and that mentally accepting the existence of God is strictly a matter of non-rational belief (faith).

As such, contemplating God's existence is erroneously regarded as the exclusive subject of faith-based or speculative ideologies (religion and philosophy) which have no proper place in natural scientific study.

The fact is, there are a number of very convincing intellectual arguments concerning the existence of God that have been around for hundreds of years. Indeed, the existence of God can be determined with compelling intellectual certainty—provided the thinker honestly wishes to do so. Moreover, recent advances and discoveries in science have not weakened previous intellectual arguments for God's existence, but instead have enormously strengthened and supported them.

Intellectually assenting to the existence of God is easily demonstrated to be a superlatively logical conclusion, not some vague irrational conceptualization. Remarkably, at the present time there are only two seriously competing intellectual explanations of life: the existence of God (the "God-hypothesis") and the existence of infinite universes (the "multiverse theory"). The postulation of an infinite number of unobservable universes is clearly a desperate attempt by atheistic scientists to avoid the God-hypothesis as the most credible and logical intellectual explanation of life and the universe. Moreover, under intellectual scrutiny, the scientifically celebrated "evolutionary theory" is here demonstrated to be fatally-flawed (philosophically illogical) as a credible explanation of life.

In this particular discourse, five well-known intellectual arguments for God's existence will be thoroughly examined. In considering these arguments, every attempt has been made to include current contributions, advances and discoveries that have modernized the more traditional arguments. Prior to examining these particular arguments for God, the universal predilection to establish intellectual 'oneness'—"monism"—will be considered in detail as well as the recurring propensity to postulate the existence of one supreme being—"monotheism."

Once intellectual certainty of one Supreme Being is established, a number of divine attributes can be logically deduced as well. Eleven of these attributes will be determined and examined in greater detail.

Also check out the authour's website:

www.heartofshambhala.com

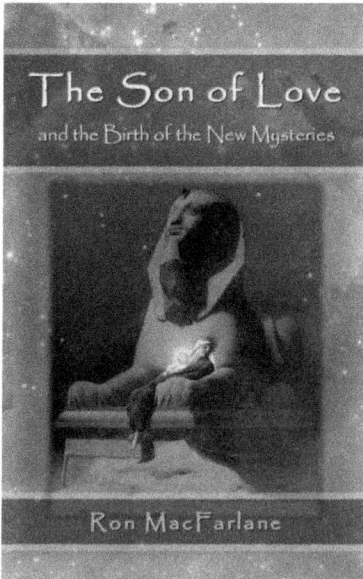

The Son of Love
and the Birth of the New Mysteries

Ron MacFarlane

FOR COUNTLESS esoteric students today, the Mystery centres of ancient times have retained a powerful and fascinating allure. Moreover, there is often a wishful longing to revive and continue their secretive initiatory activity into modern times.

Unfortunately, this anachronistic longing is largely based on an illusionary misunderstanding of these Mysteries and the real reasons for their destined demise.

The primary reason for the disappearance of the ancient Mysteries is that they have been supplanted by the superior new mysteries—the mysteries of the Son. These new mysteries were initiated by Christ-Jesus himself. In order to better understand these Son-mysteries in a spiritually-scientific way, Rudolf Steiner (1861–1925) established the Anthroposophical Movement and Society.

Unfortunately, anthroposophy today has become unduly influenced by members and leaders who long to transform spiritual science into a modern-day Mystery institution. Moreover, contrary to his own words and intentions, Rudolf Steiner is even claimed to be the founder of some new "Michael-Mysteries."

By carefully establishing a correct esoteric understanding of the ancient pagan Mysteries, as well as a better appreciation of the new mysteries of the Son, this well-researched and readable discourse convincingly shows that all current and past attempts to revive the ancient pagan Mysteries regressively diverts human development backward to the seducer of mankind, Lucifer, rather than progressively forward to the saviour of mankind, Christ-Jesus.

Moreover, by additionally tracing the intriguing historical

development of esoteric Christianity (particularly the Knights of the Holy Grail and Rosicrucianism) alongside Freemasonry, the Knights Templar and Theosophy, this important and necessary study illuminates the correct esoteric position and true significance of anthroposophical spiritual science.

This book is available to order from Amazon.com

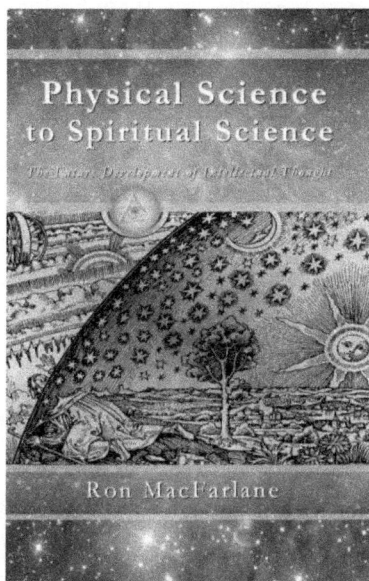

Physical Science
to Spiritual Science

The Future Development of Intellectual Thought

Ron MacFarlane

THE PRIDE OF civilized mankind—intellectual thinking—is at a critical crossroads today. No doubt surprising to many, the cognitive capacity to consciously formulate abstract ideas in the mind, and then to manipulate them according to devised rules of logic in order to acquire new knowledge has only been humanly possible for about the last 3,000 years. Prior to intellectual (abstract) thinking, mental activity characteristically consisted of vivid pictorial images that arose spontaneously in the human mind from natural and supernatural stimuli.

The ability to think abstractly is the necessary foundation for mathematics, language and empirical science. The developmental history of intellectual thought, then, exactly parallels the developmental history of mathematics, language and science. Moreover, since abstract thinking inherently encourages the cognitive separation of subject (the thinker) and object (the perceived environment), the history of intellectual development also parallels the historical development of self-conscious (ego) awareness.

Over the last 3000 years, mankind in general has slowly perfected intellectual thinking, and thereby developed complex mathematics, sophisticated languages, comprehensively-detailed empirical sciences and pronounced ego-awareness. Unfortunately, all this intellectual activity over the many previous centuries has also exclusively strengthened human awareness of the physical, material world and substantially decreased awareness of the superphysical, spiritual world.

That is why today, intellectual thinking is at a critical crossroads in further development. Thinking (intellectual or otherwise) is a superphysical activity—an activity within the soul. Empirical science is incorrect in postulating that physical brain tissue generates thought. The brain is simply the biological "sending and receiving" apparatus: sending sense-perceptions to the soul and receiving thought-conceptions from the soul. All this activity certainly generates chemical and electrical activity within the brain; but this activity is the effect, not the cause of thinking.

The danger to future intellectual thought is that increased acceptance of the erroneous scientific notion that thinking is simply brain-chemistry will increasingly deny and deaden true superphysical thinking. Future thinking runs the risk of becoming "a self-fulfilled prophecy"—the more people fervently believe that thought is simply brain-chemistry, the more thought will indeed become simply brain-chemistry. As a result, future human beings will be less responsible for generating their own thinking activity and more involuntarily controlled by their own brain chemistry. The artificial intelligence of machines won't become more human; but instead human beings will become more like robotic machines.

Presently, then, empirical science is leading intellectual thinking in a downward, materialistic direction. Correspondingly, however, true spiritual science (anthroposophy) is also actively engaged in leading intellectual thought back to its superphysical source in the soul. *From Physical Science to Spiritual Science: the Future Development of Intellectual Thought* begins by examining the historical development of intellectual thinking and the corresponding rise of physical science. Once this has been discussed, practical and detailed information is presented on how spiritual science is leading intellectual thinking back to its true soul-source. It is intended that upon completion of this discourse, sincere and open-minded readers will themselves come to experience the exhilarating, superphysical nature of their own intellectual thought.

This book is available to order from Amazon.com

Ron MacFarlane

The Star of Higher
Knowledge

The Five Guiding Mysteries of
Esoteric Christianity

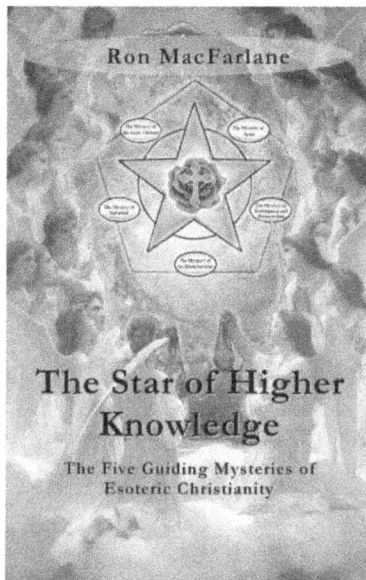

WHEN Christ-Jesus walked the earth, over two thousand years ago, he established a two-fold division in his teaching that has continued to this day. To the general public, he simplified his teaching and presented it in pictorial, allegorical and figurative imagery in the form of stories, parables and lessons that could be imaginatively and intuitively understood. To his inner circle of disciples (who were sufficiently prepared), however, he taught more plainly and directly in the form of intellectual concepts, clear ideas and logical reasoning that could be understood on a much deeper and wider level of comprehension. As biblically explained:

> Then the disciples came and said to him, "Why do you speak to them [the general public] in parables?" And he answered them, "To you it has been given to know the secrets of the kingdom of heaven, but to them it has not been given ... This is why I speak to them in parables, because seeing they do not see, and hearing they do not hear, nor do they understand." (Matt 13:10, 13)

Moreover, in union with the divine, Our Saviour was able to reveal sacred knowledge that had never been previously presented in the entire history of mankind: "I will explain mysteries hidden since the creation of the world" (Matt 13:35). This sacred and revealed knowledge has been termed, "Christ-mysteries," or "mysteries of the Son."

After his glorious resurrection and ascension, Christ-Jesus

institutionalized his two-fold mystery-teachings through St. Peter and St. John (the Evangelist, not the apostle). Through St. Peter, Our Saviour instituted a universal, Christian *religion* and *theology* to preserve, promote and convey the more basic and simplified mystery-teachings that are intended for the general public. Through St. John, Christ-Jesus instituted a universal, Christian *philosophy* and *theosophy* to preserve, promote and convey the more comprehensive and complex mystery-teachings that are intended for the more advanced disciples (Christian initiates). In esoteric terminology, the institutionalized teachings through St. Peter are known as the "lesser mysteries of exoteric Christianity." The institutionalized teachings through St. John are known as the "greater mysteries of esoteric Christianity."

While both mystery-teaching approaches are equally sacred, profound and intended to complement each other, corrupt and intolerant authorities within the universal institution (Church) of St. Peter, for many centuries, persecuted and attacked any public expressions of esoteric Christianity. Consequently, genuine historical forms of esoteric Christianity, such as the Knights of the Holy Grail and the Fraternity of the Rose-Cross, were forced to be secretive and publically-hidden during the past two thousand years.

Thankfully today, the social, political and intellectual climate has progressed to the point where the greater mystery-teachings of esoteric Christianity can begin to be publically revealed for the first time. This modern-day outpouring really began with the twentieth-century establishment of anthroposophy by Rudolf Steiner (1861–1925). The information and approach presented in *The Star of Knowledge: The Five Guiding Mysteries of Esoteric Christianity* is intended to augment and continue the mystery-teachings of Christ-Jesus as safeguarded by the Rosicrucian Fraternity and publicized through anthroposophy.

Consequently, this particular discourse delves much more deeply and comprehensively into the cosmos-changing, salvational achievement of Christ-Jesus: the historical and cosmic preparations; as well as his birth, life, death, resurrection and ascension. While much of this mystery information may be unfamiliar, unknown and unexpected to mainstream (exoteric) Christianity, it in no way is meant to criticize, denigrate or displace the profound teachings of the universal Church; but rather, to complement, to enhance and to enlarge—for the betterment of true Christianity and, thereby, the betterment of all mankind.

This book is available to order from Amazon.com

Also check out the authour's website:

www.heartofshambhala.com

A Site Dedicated to True Esoteric Christianity

www.ingramcontent.com/pod-product-compliance
Lightning Source LLC
Chambersburg PA
CBHW051728040426
42447CB00008B/1023